RADICAL ADULT EDUCATION: THEORY AND PRACTICE

J. E. Thomas

Dr. J. E. Thomas is Reader in Adult Education in the University of Nottingham, and Deputy Director of the Department of Adult Education. He has written extensively on both penology and Adult Education and is co-editor, with Dr. Peter Jarvis, of the *International Journal of Lifelong Education*. His most recent work, co-edited with Dr. Barry Elsey, is the major historical reference book *The International Biography of Adult Education*.

He was awarded the first adult education Imperial Relations Trust Bursary to study adult education in Australia and New Zealand, and has also been awarded a Fellowship of the Japan Society for the Promotion of Science, the first to an adult educator.

NOTTINGHAM STUDIES IN THE THEORY AND PRACTICE
OF THE EDUCATION OF ADULTS

RADICAL ADULT EDUCATION: THEORY AND PRACTICE

J. E. THOMAS

Reader in Adult Education
UNIVERSITY OF NOTTINGHAM

Department of Adult Education, University of Nottingham

© Department of Adult Education
University of Nottingham
1982

ISBN No: 0 902031 81 3 Paperback
ISBN No: 0 902031 87 2 Hardback

Printed by Barnes & Humby Ltd., Nottingham.

Contents

Acknowledgements

The theoretical framework which is set out in Chapter One of this book was developed, after much joint work, with Dr. Gwyn Harries-Jenkins, Deputy Director of the Department of Adult Education in the University of Hull. It was, therefore, in every sense a collaborative development, and I would like to make this clear. Dr. Harries-Jenkins has kindly agreed to my using this material, and I express my thanks to him.

I am grateful too to Mrs. Mary Emery, Publications Officer in the Department of Adult Education, University of Nottingham, for giving unfailing support. I express my appreciation of a capacity for persistence and precision in her work which is quite remarkable.

FOR JOHN, TILDA, REBECCA, AND HARRIET

Adwyn gaer yssyd
Kyweithyd o ryd wled waretret
Kynnwys rwg pop deu goreu kiwet

Introduction

Adult education, which historically has been regarded as the Cinderella of educational provision, is increasingly finding itself moving towards the centre of educational debate. This mounting interest is attributable to a number of factors. One is the rapid social and technical change which is characteristic of societies in the modern world, change which soon outdates educational experience. It soon occurs to educators that 'refreshment' is necessary. This realisation is heightened by another widespread feature of modern society, which is an incipient or actual fall in the demand for schools because of changing population patterns. This has led to a superfluity of staff and equipment in sections of the colossal education Empires which are part of the fabric of the industrial society.

Falling school populations are bound to cause professional educators to consider ways in which unused resources can be deployed. Adult education is an obvious candidate for consideration. The recognition of an increasing awareness of the importance of adult education has been demonstrated, in England, by the establishment of the Russell Committee,[1] and, as a consequence of one of its recommendations, the creation of the Advisory Council for Adult and Continuing Education.

In many countries, when scholars have been prompted to write about adult education they have, naturally, analysed and set out the history of particular facets. Much of this work is scholarly. But outside of history, much of the small amount of writing has been rather superficial. In particular, the attempt to develop any theory of adult education has been hampered by the insistence of adult educators upon debating the meaning of the term adult education. This is natural enough, since it tends to include a bewildering variety of activities. These can range from vocational training to the liberal classes of the British university tradition, and from the stimulus to national pride which is the aim of the Danish Folk High School to community education. Mention of the latter, it may be noted, provokes a whole new set of controversies about meanings.

Such discussions have become complicated in recent years by the proposal of a whole new galaxy of terms the meanings of which were soon a matter of dispute. Some of these are andragogy, *éducation permanente*, and continuing education. And there is a good deal of debate as to whether this or that activity is rightly included in this or that category. Much of this debate is sterile, many of the arguments are circular, and, on the whole little is contributed to the development of theory in respect of adult education.

This book, by starting at a different point, tries to point the way to other dimensions of the generic activity of adult education, in the expectation that intellectual discussion can be, at least potentially, more profitable. To that end, as a preliminary it is assumed that by adult education is meant the creation of opportunities for adults to learn, under the guidance of a leader, co-ordinator, or teacher. It is further assumed that an adult is someone who has finished, or is no longer eligible for, schooling. Finally, it is assumed that such activities generally take place within a structure which provides the necessary resources, and which expects adult education to achieve certain goals.

It is the nature of those goals which the theory set out in this book seeks to explore. The question which is to be raised is what adult education *achieves* or is *intended* to achieve in a particular society in which it is carried out. The emphasis will, therefore, be on the dynamic relationship between adult education and society. When policy makers, teachers, or administrators engage in the process of adult education, they are making decisions, accepting some alternatives, and rejecting others. The processes are, naturally, complex, but they do take place, and cause the establishment of adult education, in certain forms, which may later be varied, or destroyed. Inherent in the process are a host of factors — educational and social traditions, political pressures and many others.

1

This book tries to concentrate on the *action* of those concerned with adult education, since it is maintained that the making of decisions is directed towards purpose. That is not to say that there is a single purpose which applies to *all* activities, but that any given activity has a purpose which may be positive or negative: positive in the sense that it wishes to encourage change, or negative in the sense that it wishes to *prevent* change by eliminating options which could have provoked change, and substituting those which negate it.

The issues of task are clouded when discussing adult education because there is not present in the organisational process what P. L. Nokes has called a 'manifest disaster criterion'.[2] A clear example of this is bankruptcy in the commercial organisation where task failure is clearly visible. But although there is not, in a discussion of education, the luxury of such a criterion which could simplify some issues, it should be possible to explore, and generalise about, the goals of adult education in the context of a given society; and to propose a model which takes into account the relationship between the two.

To this end, the basic theoretical proposition of this book is that there is a continuum along which the activities, proposed or actual, of adult educators may be ranged. At the one extreme the activity may be classed as *radical*, at the other *conservative*. Where any given activity will be placed on the continuum will depend on three factors: its stated aims, its manifest activity, and the reaction to both of those who hold power in a society. The development of this proposition of a continuum is the essence of Chapter 1.

Chapter 2 analyses what is meant by the term 'radical adult education', suggesting that the radical seeks to destroy existing social tenets, both political *and* cultural, through education. The next chapter examines the Danish Folk High School in depth. Not only is this of intrinsic interest, but contributes to the refinement of the concept of radicalism in adult education in theory and in practice. Chapter 4 poses the intellectual problem facing all radicals: when the desired changes have been implemented, what then becomes the task of adult education? Finally, Chapter 5 suggests ways in which radical intent, or action, is contained or suppressed. I have drawn extensively upon case material from many countries to illustrate the universal nature of the debates and issues which are the concern of this book.

It will quickly become clear that many of the propositions which are made, and many of the debates which are rehearsed, are not confined to adult education. Many are generic in educational discussion, and will be of interest to a wide field of educators on that account. But, when they arise within the context of *adult* education, the debates tend to become sharper and fiercer, and therefore of more concern to those who are apprehensive about any threat to social stability.

Above all, this book raises questions about the reality of freedom in education. Is educational debate allowed to take any direction it wishes? Is the educator autonomous? Can adult students be trusted to deal wisely with any knowledge or ideas to which they are exposed? Or is the *manifest disaster criterion*, as defined by those in power, that increasing proximity of social change, which is the aim of the radical adult educator?

It should be added, as I expect will be clear to the careful reader, that I have considerable reservations about much of what radicals, of whatever persuasion, maintain as desirable goals for adult education. But I have also tried to put forward, objectively, but with force, what the radical case seems to be, in its several manifestations.

Adult educators often bewail the lack of much serious theorising about their discipline. It is to be hoped that this book will contribute to the development of the sociology of adult education.

REFERENCES

1. *Adult Education: a Plan for Development* (Chairman: Sir Lionel Russell), H.M.S.O., 1973

2. P. L. Nokes, *The Professional Task in Welfare Practice*, Routledge and Kegan Paul, 1967, pp. 7, 19-22, 112-114.

Chapter 1
A Theoretical Context

In the absence of any agreed definition of 'adult education', one of the major problems which faces any writer in this controversial field is the difficulty of looking beyond the arguments about goals, objectives and purposes. In common with other forms of education, adult education is presumed to have a specific effect on its students. Consequently, there is, in the literature on the subject, a continuing debate about what that effect should be: debate, in other words, not only about the goals or tasks of this particular form of education, but also about the more fundamental question of the relationship between adult education and the society in which its activities are carried out. Much of this discussion is common to all sections of an educational system, and the debates which have occurred in the limited area of adult studies are by no means unique. Uncertainty of purpose can be seen, for example, at the university level. Edward Gross, in his analysis of the output and support goals of eighty American universities, concluded that although a total of 47 separate goals could be identified, this figure did not mean that the list was comprehensive.[1] Many of these goals are also the goals of adult education, so that university uncertainty is repeated in the adult sector. Similarly, the debates in adult education about the merits or demerits of an examination orientated curriculum, are repeated in the secondary stage of education. In both cases, it is argued that the demands of examinations should be subordinated to the needs of social purpose, however indefinite a term this may be, or that these demands, irrespective of social purpose, should be subordinated to the dissemination of knowledge. Even the discussions at primary level, concerned with the effects of early social relationships and the events of childhood on personality, are repeated, with the substitution of 'current' for 'early' social relationships, and the replacement of 'childhood' by 'adulthood', at the adult level.

In most sectors of education, apart from adult education however, arguments are blunted and conclusions swiftly reached by the ready acceptance of defined examination or vocational goals. These, so clearly expressed and so susceptible to measurement, justify the adoption of specific maintenance or support goals, but, in total contrast, most of the activity of adult education is not orientated towards these ends. The major part of the work carried out in this field does not culminate in academic or professional validation. Indeed, there is, in many quarters, a positive opposition to the introduction of any course which seems to identify adult education with vocational training.

Several effects have followed from the adoption of this attitude. In Great Britain, and in those countries whose system of adult education has copied the British pattern, the restricted use of the term 'adult education' has, it has been alleged, caused semantic confusion and led to a deplorable neglect of the education of adults as a whole.[2] Encouraged by the narrow brief given to the 1919 Adult Education Committee, which restricted them to the consideration of 'the provision for and possibilities of adult education (other than technical or vocational)'[3] the competent sphere of activity in this field has been identified with liberal education. In Great Britain, therefore, the words 'adult education' are rarely used to describe the education of all people aged eighteen and over. In contrast with the position in the United States, where the term is more liberally interpreted to denote the education of adults as distinct from the education of children and adolescents, adult education in Britain, to both laymen and educators, means *liberal* education.

Although this restricted use of the term, recognised by the official allocation of funds for this purpose and this purpose alone,[4] has not prevented the development of a strong tradition of British adult education, several important questions remain, if not unasked, at least unanswered. Too frequently, answers have been sought in the debate about the liberal-vocational antithesis. Far too often, an assumption that the traditional type of course provided by the university extra-mural department and the Workers' Educational Association is 'superior' to those provided by other educational institutions, has created hierarchical barriers against the development of broader concepts of adult education. 'Policy-makers have been unduly concerned with liberal values and have failed to identify, let alone satisfy, practical human wants of social or economic provenance.'[5] The fundamental question of the relationship between adult education and society has, to a very large extent, been ignored. Adult education in Great Britain has remained a neglected part of the social system, a part orientated to the limited needs of a minority group, an increasing number of whom have already enjoyed the advantages of a full-time higher education.[6]

What, then, is the relationship between adult education and the society within which its activities are carried out? Is it simply a relationship between two minority groups of educated teachers and educated students, or is it a relationship between an educational elite and society as a whole? Is adult education concerned with all societal interests, or must its activities be restricted, because men are unequally endowed by nature, to a privileged group whose interests are those of individual needs and desires? These are some of the questions which this book sets out to explore further. The material brought together in this book is concerned not so much with the traditional debates of British adult education as with the wider question of the place of adult education in society. It illustrates the different interpretations of societal interests which have been put forward by a number of international writers. It also deals with the various fields of activity which are thought to be appropriate as subjects of adult education. It illustrates two important elements of an educational system, elements which are analytically separate, although they merge in concrete situations. The first consists of specifically defined goals, purposes and interests which combine to form, in Merton's words, 'a frame of aspirational reference'.[7] Some of these interests are those of society, others are more individualistic in their subjectivity, but in either case, different interpretations have been put upon them by a number of international writers. The second element under consideration comprises the activities which are thought to be appropriate in varied educational programmes. Often, these are the means whereby defined and regulated interests can, through a wide range of formal courses and less formal meetings, be implemented. Alternatively, these are the means whereby aspirations can be realized. Numerous instances occur, however, where activities, planned to be instrumental, are transformed into ends in themselves, or where from the very beginning, the concept of purpose is forgotten and activities are undertaken for the sole purpose of meeting the recreational needs of adult students.

Both types of educational activity are considered in this book, but it is the interaction between interests and activities which provides the theoretical framework for this examination of the relationship between adult education and society. Although a great part of the literature of adult education, particularly in Great Britain, is concerned with practice rather than theory, it is possible to see two interpretations of societal interests which approximate to a conflict and consensus view, respectively, of society. Conflict theorists approach the question of interests from the standpoint of the various individuals and groups within society. The needs and desires of these factions, rather than the needs of society as a whole, motivate their attitudes towards the division of power and privilege.[8] Their attitude was summed up in a review article by Talcott Parsons of C. Wright Mills' book, *The Power Elite*. Parsons commented: 'The essential point is that, to Mills, power is not a facility for the performance of function in and on behalf of the society as a system, but is interpreted exclusively as a facility for getting what one group, the holders of power, wants by preventing another group, the "outs" from getting what it wants'.[9]

4

Consensus, or functionalist, theorists, in contrast, approach the problem of societal interests from the viewpoint of society as a whole. The interests of society are then seen to be compatible with the interests of the individual, for it is the interests of the latter, as part of the whole, which govern the needs and requirements of the total social system. The cohesion, stability and persistence of this consensus model therefore emphasise, not interests and power, but the significance of norms and values which are seen to be the basic elements of social life. To these theorists, adult education is not a facility for promoting the social policies of a particular group, but is a means of transmitting the inherited knowledge and culture of the whole society. Value-judgements are then concerned with cognitive rather than social or political values.

Despite a widespread criticism of these consensus/conflict models of society, a criticism which has become one of the principal issues in the recent literature of social theory,[10] both theories have a particular relevance in the analysis of the relationship between adult education and society. The nature of individual interests, as they are interpreted by supporters of the conflict model of society, suggests that to the mature adult, education is seen as a means whereby the power, prestige and privilege of the individual can be increased. More importantly, the identification of the conflict model with the proposition that social systems tend to change, encourages the belief that adult education is primarily a vehicle of change. This concept of adult education as a radical force, seeking to make a major impact on society, means that an education programme is only valid or viable if it seems to challenge basic assumptions about socio-economic structures, value systems, and cultural and aesthetic norms. There is a total rejection of any interpretation of the goals of adult education which identifies these goals with the maintenance of the existing social system.

Supporters of the consensus model, by far the majority of adult educators, believe that adult education has no rôle as an instigator or supporter of change. Society, that is its structures, value systems and norms, is therefore accepted as a static framework which provides the boundaries within which the activities of adult education should be carried out. From this point of view, it is not the primary task of adult education to challenge the validity of this framework, although such a challenge *may* arise as a result of the effect of education on societal interests.

If such a challenge does not occur, this does not reduce the intrinsic value of a devised teaching programme, for the essential question is whether the transmitted knowledge has been educationally worthwhile.

In addition to the effect of this consensus/conflict interpretation of social interest on attitudes towards the relationship between adult education and change, a second determinant of attitudes is the distinction between value-orientated and norm-orientated perceptions. This distinction has been clearly brought out by Smelser who has shown how a value-orientated organisation is directed towards changes in the generalised ends or values that a social order is designed to achieve. Conversely, a norm-orientated organisation seeks to retain existing goals although it aims to change the rules that govern the *pursuit* of basic objectives and the detailed operation of basic forms of social order.[11] The contrast is between revolution and reform and in this context the rôle of adult education is of critical importance. By themselves, for example, values and norms do not determine who will be agents in the pursuit of valued ends, or how the action of these agents will be structured into concrete rôles and organisations. It is the 'mobilisation of motivation into organised action' which is of fundamental significance, and here adult education is of importance for two reasons. In the first place, it provides the *structure* by which this mobilisation can be achieved, creating a community of association which exercises moral, intellectual and, if needed, forcible control over the society which supports it. In some ways it has a rôle which has been termed that of the 'secular church'[12], for where it is value-orientated, the purpose of the community is seen to be that of 'meditating' on the state of society and of then promoting change. In contrast, the importance of the structure, where it is norm-orientated, is derived from the cybernetic role of adult education. Here, the perceived responsibility for conserving and elaborating the higher cultural standards of society ensure that adult education organisations exercise a form of control whereby the criteria of normative standards are applied in the solution of contemporary problems.

Some supporters of the consensus model claim, nevertheless, that their propositions about the rôle of adult education in society do subscribe to social purpose as a goal. This is illustrated in several ways. One dominant conception, inspired by the arguments of men such as Albert Mansbridge, the founder and first secretary of the W.E.A., asserts that the mass of ordinary men and women need a humane education as such, an education which can be turned to good account.[13] Adult educators, who subscribe to this interpretation of the objectives of education, hope, by introducing students to cultural treasures, to contribute to the development of a richer, fuller personality. They want to help in the production of the classical 'cultured man'. In Tawney's words, written in 1914, 'The first task of any such society as the Workers' Educational Association is to lay to rest that smiling illusion which whispers that 'culture' is something that one class—'the educated'—possess, that another—'the uneducated'—are without, and that the former, when sufficiently warmed by sympathy or alarm, can transfer to the latter in pills made up for weak digestions'.[14] In turn, it is believed that there will follow from this a more mature and sensitive approach to life and society, an approach which is not the prerogative of any single faction within that society.

A second concept is derived from the belief that the idea of social solidarity has an educational, as well as a political or economic, base. This again presumes that individual or sectional interests are subordinate to societal needs—'the surprising fact that there is no inconsiderable number of men and women whose incentive to education is not material success but spiritual energy, and who seek it, not in order that they may become something else, but because they are what they are'.[15] The idea of social solidarity is thus a key factor in this consensus model of society, for solidarity implies a general willingness to accept the norms and values which create the fundamental unity and cohesion of society.

From this, it follows that social problems must be considered within the existing framework of society. In finding solutions, the importance of adult education can be attributed to the consensus thesis that the occupancy of key positions in society is evidence of superior ability. Whereas a conflict theorist rejects the existing status hierarchy, the consensus theorist accepts the hierarchy but wants to ensure that *la carrière ouverte aux talents* is accompanied by *égalité de fait*. This equality of opportunity and universality of provision can be ensured, through the extension of educational opportunities to all sections of society through the medium of adult education programmes. By this means, the functions of problem-solving and decision-making are no longer the prerogatives of a small minority, but are exercisable by all members of society.

The distinction between these two interpretations of the relationship between adult education and society is, however, rarely expressed in terms of polar extremes. The concepts of adult education as a radical force, primarily seeking to make a major impact on society, or as a conservative force, orientated towards the atomistic view of man, are graduated. They are, therefore, best seen as parts of a continuum. At one extreme is the view that any system of adult education, which is to be effective, must challenge established economic and social assumptions. At the other, is the view that adult education contributes to the preservation of the existing system. Between these positions, there are a number of less extreme views, the boundaries of which are often blurred so that no position is exclusive. If

6

these views are analysed, it can be suggested that interpretations of the relationship between adult education and society can be grouped under the four headings of *revolution, reform, maintenance* and *conservation*. The characteristics of each group shade into those of its neighbour on the continuum, but each group displays certain distinct and peculiar features.

The interests which can be subsumed under the heading of *revolution* are essentially derived from the conflict model of society. These, as I have noted, are primarily individual or group orientated, so that one criticism which can be made of this interpretation of the link between adult education and society is that it is derived from the 'inflamed ambition of individuals'.[16] An interesting corollary of this criticism identifies 'revolution' with an innate radicalism, and this association seems to be generally accepted. It must be noted, however, that a belief in a justified social revolution need not be exclusively 'radical' in character. As Barrington Moore has pointed out, revolution can also emanate from 'Above'.[17] In this respect, adult education can be used as a vehicle for encouraging or endorsing a fascist revolution through the conscious manipulation of the public mind to create, as in Italy and Germany during the 1930's, ready acceptance of postulated ideological doctrines.[18] In either case, however, irrespective of the precise political connotation which can be attributed to this concept of revolution, adult education continues to be identified with ideas of individual or group advantage.

Although this concept is in no way a new phenomenon, it is noticeable that it is no longer interpreted simply as a specific concept concerned only with political events and goals. Instead, it has become an unstructured concept representing an idealized pattern of social relationships. 'The idea of violence, unpredictability, the overthrow of the powerful, resistance to domination, and independence remained. But in the new synthesis revolution was much more. It was youth defying age, liberation from the population explosion and social constraints, achieving the impossible, a formula for re-shaping the world in any image, internal or external.'[19] This, then, is the revolution of social engineering or social upheaval. It is Emerson's 'do your own thing'[20] or Johnson's 'millenarian rebellion',[21] situations in which the objectives of adult education programmes are seen to be the need to challenge basic assumptions about society, and the need to encourage *stasis* or social dissolution.

In contrast with this contemporary interpretation of the nature of revolution, the concept of *reform* seems to be more closely linked with an historical past. While it too is concerned with changes within society, many of its characteristics are reminiscent of comments which were made in the nineteenth century. It would be incorrect to identify the concept solely with these early theories of social revolution, but this interpretation of the relationship between adult education and society owes a great deal to the nineteenth century model. Paine's defence of the French Revolution, for example, remains a very apt comment on this concept of reform. It is, in his words, 'a renovation of the natural order of things, a system of principles as universal as truth and the existence of man, and combining moral with political happiness and national prosperity'.[22] Indeed, in many ways, the movement for reform can be seen 'not as the initiative of a new age, but as the last formula of an expiring age'.[23]

In adult education circles, this concept of reform is a very popular one. It is attractive, for example, to those liberals who, while they reject the validity of the consensus model of society, are not prepared to endorse a revolutionary appeal for total social dissolution. It continues to be based on an awareness of individual or group interests, but these are now interpreted as a complex symbiotic relationship between members of interest groups. The latter possess 'affinities of interest', arising from sources as diverse as 'relations of kinship, the division of labour, exchanges in the market place, and the ubiquitous influence of custom'.[24] The interest groups which are thereby formed, reflect the differences in their goals. Political

7

parties, the military, business groups, trade unions, and organised pressure groups are all representative of an amorphous power structure.

The attraction of these groups to adult educators is derived from a realisation that these groups are dynamic rather than static. Adult education can then be clearly seen to have a purpose. On the one hand, it can press for reforms in the structure of these groups, using adult education programmes as a social dynamic, while not challenging the assumptions which legitimize the existence of these groups. Alternatively, it can prepare students for membership of these groups, preparing them for the exercise of social duties and responsibilities, and encouraging their educational and social mobility. These groups are also attractive because they can be conceived as *veto-groups*, each of which is primarily concerned with protecting its jurisdiction by blocking the action of other groups which seem to threaten it.[25] This interpretation minimises the effect of conflict, in the sense that conflict can be defined as the elimination of an opposition to achieve a given goal, and substitutes instead the idea of competition. Once again, this gives a sense of purpose to adult education programmes. Life can now be seen to be 'a series of hurdle-jumps, the hurdles of scholarships which are won by learning to amass and manipulate the new currency'.[26] The principles of competition, the idea of the career open to talent, and the desire to create a just open society, emphasise the value of the contribution which adult education can make to the development of individual personality.

Popular endorsement of the merits of this reform movement is not based, however, simply on the attractiveness of the theory of interest groups. In Great Britain, the demand for reform has a lengthy history and it has been encouraged in a wide variety of situations. While the concept of revolution is primarily associated with political movements and ideologies, that of reform is much more widely based. The latter can be seen, for example, in the traditions of Christian democracy for which Mansbridge stood in the W.E.A. Out of the alliance of the adult schools and the Quakers, there stemmed the educational settlements[27] with their own theories of reforming the insular, the sectarian and the personal.[28] This stirring of the social conscience was echoed, particularly in the years between 1919 and 1939, in a wide number of other educational institutions. The tragedy of much of this reform movement, however, was that somewhere along the way it lost direction. Too much time was spent in debating problems of organization or administration: too little time was spent in considering the need to relate contemporary social developments to traditional areas of concern.[29]

One effect of this was to blur the boundaries between the *reform* and *maintenance* interpretation of the relationship of adult education to society. In theory, there are important distinctions between these two interpretations. The concept of reform is based on a conflict theory of society, whereas the concept of maintenance draws its inspiration from the opposing consensus model. In practice, however, it may be difficult to identify the particular characteristics which are usually attributed to the two models in question. This can be seen in a number of examples. Supporters of the reform concept thus argue that their primary concern is with society as a whole, not the interests of any specific group, although the reform/conflict thesis is essentially based on the idea of sectional interests. Conversely, the maintenance concept, theoretically based on the needs of society as a whole, may be interpreted to mean the wish to create a stable society for the continuing advantages of particular interests or groups.

The third example is perhaps more important. Consensus, it is argued, does not necessarily mean persistence as opposed to change. There may be, as Cohen has pointed out, 'consensus on the direction and forms of change'.[30] Similarly, the absence of consensus, or the placing of an undue emphasis on the interests of a particular group, may create a dysfunctional situation which, through the emergence of an impasse, prevents or inhibits

8

planned change. A final example emphasises the theoretical difficulties which occur. The concept of maintenance is based on the idea of social integration, relying on the consensus, solidarity or cohesion which are characteristics of the consensus model of society. But, as Lockwood argues, integration may well be applicable to societies with structured conflict, since the latter ensures the functional interrelationship of the various parts of the social structure.[31] In this sense, therefore, the idea of integration cannot be regarded as an exclusive characteristic of the maintenance/consensus model, since it may be found in the reform/conflict model.

Although the difficulty of reconciling these criticisms with the postulated characteristics of the two models of society is very evident in the extensive literature on the subject, it is important to remember that the creation of the models owes a great deal to ideology.[32] For the adult educators, therefore, their importance is derived not from their methodological correctness, but from the reasoned ideological arguments which underlie the defence of either or both of the two models. One effect of this, is that the concept of maintenance, as it is interpreted by the supporters of this idea of the relationship between adult education and society, is associated with a wish to maintain the existence of those norms which are considered to be the basis of social life. They are particularly involved in the maintenance of the underlying system or values which influence the norms to be found throughout society. There is thus ample evidence of a developed interest, not only in ensuring a sense of commitment to those norms, but also in creating consensus on the values which produce them. The most suitable situation for ensuring the development of adult education programmes orientated to these ends is found, it is believed, in a stable social system which encourages the maintenance of the status quo. Here, the formulation of societal goals, in terms of the accepted norms and the creation of a harmonious sense of values, encourages the creation of teaching programmes which are specifically designed to encourage social integration.

The possibility of change is not excluded from consideration. To be accepted as valid, however, this must be a planned change which arises as society, as a whole, adapts to universally accepted amendments to existing norms and values. Changes which are reflections of sectional interests are disregarded, on the grounds that these do not contribute towards the maintenance of the whole. A resulting preoccupation with the believed needs of society can be discerned in most discussions about the rôle of adult education in relation to socio-cultural factors. Among these, for example, a frequent cause of controversy arises from the postulated need to produce a large number of educated specialists who can fill appointments as administrators, professionals and managers. It is here that the liberal versus vocational argument is most frequently waged, although the force of the arguments used are weakened by the general agreement that there is a need to achieve a synthesis between the two conceptions of a literary or technical culture.

A second social need, which, it is argued, can be filled through the medium of adult education programmes, is the requirement of society for 'productive workers who enjoy their lives. This means the most economical and effective use of man-power, and it also means that happiness is a factor in efficiency'.[33] The implications of this as an educational goal are far-reaching. For many employers of labour, it endorses their belief in a custodial model of organizational behaviour, in which the natural measure of morale is employee satisfaction.[34] Consequently, they approve or support adult education activities which contribute to the development of employee maintenance needs and increase the latter's organizational dependency. Concomitantly, they reject the validity of courses which are based on the premises of reform or revolution, and, in certain circumstances, the employer can actively oppose the establishment or continuation of 'radical' adult education programmes.[35]

A belief that this goal of individual happiness is best satisfied in the maintenance model through programmes which are based on established norms and values, creates several problem areas. A bipartite system of adult education may be created in which 'recreational' programmes, designed to promote a general liberal education, are sharply distinguished from 'reparative' or 'renovative' courses.[36] It is disputed whether these latter courses properly fall within the province of the university extra-mural department and the established bodies. At the same time, 'liberal' is narrowly defined to exclude many of the courses which are held in evening institutes, so that the concept of happiness or social needs is interpreted to mean these concepts, as they are interpreted by the educational elite. Indeed, the very idea of maintenance presumes that it is only an elite who can best judge the type of education which is required to ensure the continued stability of society. In short, maintenance is tutor rather than student orientated, for individual requirements must be subordinated to the believed needs of society.

The emphasis which is placed in the maintenance model on the stability of society, is carried a stage further in the *conservation* model, for here there is a total rejection of change. Whereas it is accepted in the maintenance model that planned change may be a necessary corollary of stability, conservationists adopt a stance which is opposed to any association of adult education with changes within society. This includes the rejection of any courses which may be defined as renovative, that is, designed to retrain qualified individuals, as well as courses which can be more directly associated with reform or revolution. In the conservation model, the aims of adult education are seen as the need to protect the traditional subjects of study from change, and the need to uphold an elite tradition in education.

The justification for the retention of this model is largely based on out-moded conceptions of education as something which is gentlemanly, non-utilitarian and largely ornamental. The goal of this model was admirably summed up by T. S. Eliot when he wrote that 'The first task of the communities should be the preservation of education within the cloisters uncontaminated by the deluge of barbarism outside'.[37] Eliot, however, was not alone in his interpretation of the goals of education, and a common theme among adult educationists who are supporters of the conservation model is their dislike of a contemporary 'mechanized, commercialized, industrialized existence'.[38]

The arguments which have been used to justify the existence of this model have been admirably analysed by Flann Campbell, although it would be incorrect to interpret his comments on 'Latin and the Elite Tradition in Education'[39] to mean that conservation in adult education is only concerned with the teaching of classics. His analysis of the elite tradition in education shows how, apart from the linguistic and aesthetic aspects of the classics, this tradition is orientated towards the identification of education with training for leadership. From this doctrine, and on the basis of the faculty theory of psychology, which claimed that what was important in teaching a subject was not so much interest or relevance, but formal training and mental discipline, 'flowed the theory that in adult life the liberally educated amateur was to be preferred to the vocationally-trained specialist'.[40] Accordingly, the conservation model in adult education continues to emphasise the need for courses which encourage the acquisition of mental skills which, it is alleged, can be applied or transferred to other academic skills, and carried over to mundane problems of professional or managerial life.[41]

REFERENCES

1. Edward Gross, 'The Definition of Organizational Goals', *British Journal of Sociology* Vol. XX, No. 3, September 1969, pp. 277-294, at p. 287.

2. John Lowe, *Adult Education in England and Wales: a Critical Survey*, Michael Joseph, 1970, p. 23.

3. Ministry of Reconstruction, *Final Report of the Adult Education Committee*. H.M.S.O., 1919. Sometimes called '*The Smith Report*', but more usually referred to as '*The 1919 Report*'. An abridged version with an editorial introduction was published in 1956. Cf. R. D. Waller (ed.), *A Design for Democracy*, Parrish, 1956. The complete report has been republished as H. Wiltshire, J. Taylor and B. Jennings *The 1919 Report: the Final and Interim Reports of the Adult Education Committee of the Ministry of Reconstruction 1918-1919*, Department of Adult Education, University of Nottingham, 1980. The Board of Education's regulations, and their effect on the development of adult education in England, are analysed in S. G. Raybould, *The English Universities and Adult Education*, W.E.A., 1951, Appendices I and III.

4. Cf. S. G. Raybould, *University Extra-Mural Education in England 1945-62: a Study in Finance and Policy*, Michael Joseph, 1964, pp. 20-21.

5. Lowe, op. cit., p. 27.

6. A number of studies have analysed the previous educational attainment of adult education students. The generally reached conclusion is that an increasing number of students have enjoyed the advantages of a higher education before entering upon subsequent adult education courses. Cf. B. W. Pashley, *University Extension Reconsidered*, Leicester University (Vaughan College Paper No. 11), 1968; Lowe, op. cit., Appendices 2 and 3; National Institute of Adult Education, *Adult Education—Adequacy of Provision*, N.I.A.E., 1970; J. W. C. Johnstone and R. J. Rivera, *Volunteers for Learning*, Chicago, Aldine Publishing Company, 1965.

7. Robert K. Merton, 'Social Structure and Anomie', *American Sociological Review*, Vol. 3, 1938, pp. 672-680 at p. 673.

8. Cf. Gerhard E. Lenski, *Power and Privilege*, New York, McGraw-Hill, 1966, pp. 16-17.

9. Talcott Parsons, 'The Distribution of Power in American Society', *World Politics*, Vol. 10, October 1957, p. 139.

10. Cf. Percy Cohen, *Modern Social Theory*, Heinemann, 1968, pp. 166-167.

11. Neil J. Smelser, *Theory of Collective Behaviour*, New York, Routledge, 1962, p. 26.

12. Guy E. Swanson, *Social Change*, Glenview, Illinois, Scott, Foresman, 1971, p. 166.

13. Cited in R. H. Tawney, *The Radical Tradition*, Penguin, 1966, p. 89.

14. Ibid., p. 81.

15. Ibid., p. 78.

16. Ibid., p. 78.

17. Barrington Moore, *Social Origins of Dictatorship and Democracy*, Penguin, 1967, Chapter Eight.

18. For an analysis of the part played by adult education in furthering fascist ideology in Italy during the 1930s, cf. E. J. Jones, *Some Aspects of Adult Education in Italy*, London, World Association for Adult Education, 1934.

19. Peter Calvert, *Revolution*, Pall Mall, 1970, p. 109.

20. Ralph Waldo Emerson, 'Self-Reliance', in *Essays, First and Second Series*, New York, Macmillan, 1885, p. 33.

21. Chalmers Johnson, *Revolution and the Social System*, U.S.A. Hoover Institute Press, 1964, p. 153.

22. Thomas Paine, *Rights of Man. Being an Answer to Mr. Burke's Attack on the French Revolution*, London, 1930, p. 135.

23. This is Mazzini's comment on the French Revolution: Cf. Giuseppi Mazzini, *The Duties of Man and Other Essays by Joseph Mazzini*, London, 1912, p. 251.

24. Reinhard Bendix, 'Social Stratification and Political Community', in Reinhard Bendix and Seymour Martin Lipset (eds.), *Class Status and Power*, Routledge, 1967, p. 84.

25. The concept of *veto-groups* is elaborated in David Riesman, *The Lonely Crowd*, New York, Yale University Press, 1953, pp. 257-258.

26. Richard Hoggart, *The Uses of Literacy*, Penguin, 1969, p. 297.

27. The history of educational settlements in England is summarised in Thomas Kelly, *A History of Adult Education in Great Britain*, Liverpool University Press, 1962, pp. 261-263.

28. H. Fleming, 'Education through Settlements', Birkenhead, *Beechcroft Bulletin* No. 2, 1922, p. 5.

29. Pre-occupation in the inter-war years with problems of organization and administration can be noted in contemporary issues of *The Tutor's Bulletin*, published by the Association of Tutorial Class Tutors. In August 1926, for example, the *Bulletin* is concerned with the questions 'Should joint committees run one-year classes?' and with 'The Organization of Tutorial Class Work in London'. The report in this issue of the 1926 Annual

11

Conference at Easton Lodge shows that, of the five sessions which were held, four were concerned with topics which dealt with the administrative problems of holding one-year classes, organizing the extra-mural department of a university, the appointment of tutors and the effectiveness of W.E.A. organization. The report of the fifth session on the 'Teaching of Psychology' shows how great was the concern with standards, and the relationship of the 'new psychology' to traditional liberal subjects.

30. Cohen, op. cit., p. 271.

31. David Lockwood, 'Social Integration and System Integration', in George G. K. Zollschan and Walter Hirsch (eds.), *Exploration in Social Change*, Routledge and Kegan Paul, 1964, pp. 244-256.

32. Cohen, op. cit., p. 171.

33. A. K. C. Ottaway, *Education and Society*, Routledge, 1953, p. 92.

34. Cf. Keith Davis, *Human Relations at Work: the Dynamics of Organizational Behaviour*, New York, McGraw-Hill, 1967, for an elaboration of the characteristics of this custodial model, one of four models which he conceptualized as tools to explore further behaviour within organizations.

35. Cf. Phillips Bradley, 'The University's Role in Workers' Education', *Adult Education Journal*, Vol. 8, No. 83, April 1949, and 'Commission of Inquiry on the Workers Educational Service of the University of Michigan', *Report and Recommendations*, Detroit, Michigan Committee on Civil Rights, 1949.

36. These terms are those used by A. John Allaway, *Thought and Action in Extra-Mural Work, Leicester, 1946-1966*, Leicester University (Vaughan, College Paper No. 10), 1967. The object of *reparative* courses is to introduce those, who have never previously had the opportunity, to courses of a university character. *Renovative* courses are aimed at helping the educationally and professionally qualified to familiarise themselves with new developments in their field of interest.

37. T. S. Eliot, *Essays Ancient and Modern*, Faber & Faber, 1949.

38. R. W. Livingstone, *Greek Ideals and Modern Life*, Oxford University Press, 1935, p. 115.

39. Flann Campbell, 'Latin and the Elite Tradition in Education', in *The British Journal of Sociology*, Vol. XIX, No. 3, September 1968, pp. 308-325.

40. Ibid, p. 313.

41. The belief, that acquired mental skills can be transferred to other areas of study, is admirably expressed in statements which are made to defend the inclusion of the classics in an educational curriculum. Thus, A. N. Whitehead argued that 'if ever in after life your job is to think, render thanks to Providence which ordained that, for five years of your youth, you did a Latin prose once a week, and daily construed some Latin author' A. N. Whitehead, *The Aims of Education*, Benn, 1962, p. 100.

Chapter 2
Radical Adult Education

This book is concerned with the radical end of the theoretical continuum which has been described. This analysis takes as its starting point the fact that society is held together by a network of values, myths, rôles, and structures. On the whole, most people share the same values most of the time, otherwise the society would disintegrate. To ensure stability, societies set limits on the kinds of behaviour which are tolerable, and arrange a set of sanctions for those who break those limits. The boundaries set are arbitrary, and not generally based on any eternal values, although one of the main functions of the social myth is to insist that certain boundaries are timeless and universal. It is a commonplace that some acts of today which are reprehensible, and even illegal, may, tomorrow, be tolerated, or even approved.

So it is that many of the 'debates' about religion, education, the rôle of the social worker, and the rest, take place within the constricting limits of boundaries set by social mythologies. When teachers discuss education, they talk about staff appointments and structures, ill discipline, and other everyday problems. There is very little talk of finding an alternative to schools since school is inevitable. To suggest its abolition is to break a boundary. Teachers are by no means alone in this. Social workers, prison officers, doctors, university professors are much occupied with trying to improve existing systems which, it is assumed, are basically sound. The radical approach is to question the very assumptions on which organisations, institutions, and society itself, rest. The radical claims that the wrong questions are asked, mainly because they are not sufficiently basic. The question should not be how best universities can work, but whether there should be universities at all. Radical comes to mean therefore 'change at the base' as Barrow defines it in his critique of radical alternatives to school.[1] To put it another way, radicalism is the expressed intention to attack the foundations of a system, complemented by a visible, manifest effort to do so, whether or not that effort is successful.[2] The number of writers on education who may be classed as radical in this sense is very small; the number of *practitioners* in any radical endeavour is even smaller. In this respect, the distinction between adult and school education is slight. Although the radical rôle of adult education is a popular topic in professional debate, very few people actually do very much to practise it.

The radicals would say that those who prefer a comprehensive system of schooling to a grammar school system are not radical at all: they are tinkering with the problem. The adult educator who advocates more community development is not radical either. The radical wishes to question social 'limits'—political, social, and cultural, and, usually, to destroy them. That such a policy has not been attractive to large numbers of adult educators is hardly surprising. Most are concerned with the transmission of politically neutral information about practical skills, and cannot see what such a job has to do with the structure and goals of society. Some have thought about it, and disapprove of the radical view. Freire claims that people such as teachers are infused with the oppressor mentality, which means that they want, however 'rational' their arguments may be, to perpetuate the system which brings them such power and comfort. This is at least a tempting explanation for one of the most remarkable features of British university life: an almost universal refusal, until recently to allow part-time students the facilities to gain degrees. Any study of the relationship between university and community in Britain could well take, as its starting point, the fact that, for almost half the year, some of the best facilities in the country lie idle.

So, in the literature of education in general, and adult education in particular, there is not a great deal which may be called radical. In British writing at the present time, there is little of any substance, which in itself is a fact replete with interest. Such writing as there has been in earlier times in Britain and elsewhere, and recently in other countries, is important, controversial, and in sum, still relevant. The attacks launched by radicals make non radicals very angry. In conventional education circles the names of Illich or Freire excite very strong feelings indeed. Radical critics, though small in number, are difficult to ignore.

The origins of radical criticism in respect of adult education lie in two events which were roughly contemporary. These were the rise and growth of adult education, and the writings of Marx and Marxists. The 'extension' development in the nineteenth century universities, the establishment of the Workers' Educational Association, and similar ventures were paralleled by the most fevered debates about society and its institutions, inspired by the Marxists. It was not long before the growth of adult education, social discontent and unrest, and Marxism, became connected. To the debate about the desirability or otherwise of 'utility' in education there was now added a new, and more significant discussion. What was the *broad* aim of education in relation to society and its values? And what was, or should be, the commitment of adult education to that aim? This was the question which interested left wing radical adult educators, especially in the early years of this century and which expressed itself in the conflict at Ruskin College, Oxford, which will be discussed later.

The Marxist proposition insofar as it is relevant to adult education is simple. Briefly, it is that the heart of capitalist society is the economic system, which is maintained by the existence of two groups: the bourgeoisie, and the proletariat. This central nub is termed the 'substructure'. Holding this substructure intact is another, called the 'superstructure'. The latter is made up of a number of devices, all of which are devoted to the maintenance of the status quo, and the inhibition of change. These devices include law, religion, and, of course, education. Thus education is not a grand, abstracted, search for truth, regardless of where it may be found, but is, instead, a tool used to shore up the capitalist system.

It is easy to see how such an interpretation gave to the radical an intelligible explanation of educational history. The reasons why the nineteenth century saw a growth in schooling and in adult education were twofold. First, there was the purely functional need for people who were literate and skilled. This functional motive has always been the predominant force for educational change. Acknowledgement of the functional task leads to the conclusion that there was little idealism behind the major educational Acts of the century, or the growth of, for example, Mechanics' Institutes. They were intended to fulfil the need for greater skills, which industrialisation had called into being. The second explanation for the extension of education to the masses was more subtle and more insidious. It was, as one wrote:

'to educate the wage workers in being good "citizens" (e.g. wageworkers) of capitalism.'[3]

The radicals were baffled as to why there should be any dispute about this. After all, they argued, the reality is that capitalist governments, dominated by capitalists, can be expected to maintain capitalism, and to use every means, especially the enormously powerful one of education, to achieve that end. And, 'it is not' as the Australian 'Ivan the Fool' noted in 1918, 'the habit of governments to give anything for nothing'. He summed up the views of most radicals, when he opined that the whole of liberal education was 'all part of a gigantic conspiracy of benevolence'.[4]

The clarity which the radicals ascribed to such self-evident truths posed a problem for them. If the rôle of education is so apparent, why was it not clear to working class people that they were being duped? Put simply, the radical answer is that they are moulded by the system and cannot, at first, identify the reality of their situation. Because people are nurtured on certain assumptions about the inevitability of particular social systems, so they

14

are numbed by them. The fact that, in the early years of this century, substantial numbers of the working class were pro capitalist, as indeed is still the case, is regrettable, even depressing, but quite understandable. It is:

> 'because of the enormously powerful control exercised by the employing class over the thoughts of the workers through the medium of the press, the schools, the universities, the cinema, and similar institutions.'[5]

The process begins early, and the worker 'may be caught young and have his teeth drawn by the operation of free and compulsory primary education'.[6] Eventually he will be:

> 'well indoctrinated with the rudiments of imperialism, rationalism, and any other branches of learning needed by those who are to enter early on the career of a wage slave.'[7]

The process goes on until 'a docile and contented proletariat' is formed, 'and the capitalist system will work as smoothly as a shark's jaws'.[8]

This analogy between education, power, and the jaws of sharks is something of a favourite with radical writers. Reimer in *School is dead*, quotes at length an extract from Brecht in which the sharks school the little fish into accepting a world which operates for the benefit of the sharks. The prospect of ending such a system becomes terrifying to its victims, and instilled into them is the fear of freedom which makes the termination of slavery so difficult to achieve.[9]

It is often claimed by radicals that the surest proof of the use of education by those with power to maintain that power can be seen from the placid, uncritical, acceptance by people of the unpleasantness of much modern life. Reimer, again, is representative:

> 'An educated minority of any size would never put up with current health and education services, environmental pollution, political policy control by military-industrial cliques or advertiser control of mass media, to say nothing of traffic jams, housing shortages and the host of other absurdities which afflict modern societies.'[10]

Adult education is a particular target for the radicals, since, they claim, its rôle is to mop up any potential dissidents who may have escaped the educational treadwheel. There will always be such people, and, to cope with them, there are the institutions of the adult educators. But the rôle of these institutions is to castrate; to reduce, and ideally eliminate, the anger engendered by experience of an elitist education system; to neutralise any determination to set matters right; and to recruit such ability as there may be, for the system. Even those who failed, yet had ability, were vulnerable, since they had ingrained in them the same respect for education and its institutions as everyone else. There is:

> 'nothing like education to draw away peoples' interest and sympathy from the wrongs and sorrows of the actual into an atmosphere of foggy and abstract idealism! Nothing like a little learning to minister to pride, egotism and selfish ambition!'[11]

Such tactics are enormously successful, with Australian workers on the one hand declining to take part in celebrations to mark the anniversary of the Russian revolution, and on the other being 'dazzled' by the presence of university professors. This was a culmination of what Illich describes as 'an enforced stay in the company of teachers which pays off in the doubtful privilege of more such company'.[12]

This then was how the earlier radical critics of adult education perceived its development. The institutions, from Australian branches of the W.E.A. to Ruskin College, Oxford, were simply parts of the superstructure. They were not as manifestly coercive as the machinery of criminal justice, but were more sinister, and much more sophisticated. The success of all could be measured by the existence of a pliant working class which believed that capitalism and its attendants, such as imperialism, were immutable and desirable.

15

Workers happily accepted the boundaries of intellectual enquiry delineated by the rulers, and enjoyed the education which was packaged for them.

The early history of Ruskin is a classic example of these stresses. When it was established, its purpose seemed to be clear enough. The idea was, in essence, to provide opportunities for the spreading of university educational experience to those people who, in earlier times, would have had no chance of gaining it. The aims of Ruskin were consonant with the assumptions of the emerging adult education of the time, as it was expressed in the Extension movement, and the W.E.A. The expectation of the adult educational Establishment of the time was summed up by the Liberal leader Campbell-Bannerman, who observed that Ruskin 'will give precisely the learning and inspire precisely the sort of spirit which is desired, without an unduly disturbing influence on those who are subject to it'.[13]

By 1907 the numbers of students who had nevertheless been 'disturbed' by their experience was growing, and very soon quarrels developed about the ideological content, or what might be today called the 'hidden curriculum', of the course material. The students, being mature, and generally with socialist backgrounds, refused to submit to the demands made by the authorities. As a consequence of a meeting in 1908, the Plebs League, as it was later known, was formed. Its object was to develop links between Ruskin and the Labour Movement. In 1909, a Central Labour College was established in Oxford, which sought support from the Labour Movement and established an educational network which aimed at serving the Movement.

Like the Ruskin rebels, those who subscribed to a revolutionary purpose for adult education rejected boundaries which they believed bolstered an unequal and depriving regime. But they did not only disapprove because they disliked capitalism (which they did) but because they believed that the education purveyed by the system distorted the very Truth with which, allegedly, education was concerned. They did not, therefore, see education as a crude tool with which to capture power. Rather did they believe that if education really did occupy itself with Truth, then the capitalist system would collapse. It was not just a revolutionary tactic, such as gaining control of the Army, or of the broadcasting station, might be. It was, at its most idealistic, a desire to introduce honesty and *real* enquiry into the educational process: a constant theme in radical critiques, not only of adult education, but of education generally. This idealism is, it is suggested, expressed, typically, by Reimer:

'True education is a basic social force. Present social structures could not survive an educated population, even if only a substantial minority were educated . . . People are schooled to accept a society. They are educated to create or recreate one.'[14]

Such radicals' optimism about the effectiveness of 'true' education is considerable, as when Reimer claims:

'Class distinctions would also tend to disappear in educated societies . . .'[15]

In the same way Sarup detects high expectations of education as a force for change:

'. . . The main object of the "new" sociology of education is the attempt to make the world better, the realisation of a free and equal society in which dialogue would be the ideal form of relationship. Grounded in a vision of a just society, this view entails de-reification of the world of education.'[16]

Reactionary resistance to this vision is subtle. The Horrabins examine, for example, the concept of the much vaunted 'liberal education'. This they traced back to the Greek idea of education which was 'appropriate for a freeman who was supported by slaves and who had before him a life of leisure'.[17] This 'ruling class conception' is irrelevant to the needs of workers, and is unintelligible to them. What is interesting to them are 'studies which have a

16

practical bearing on their own needs and aspirations'.[18] Such studies would encourage an awareness of the lack of freedom in the condition of the working class. This is not, the radicals claim, propaganda, but an inevitable result of the search for truth.

The argument that education has a social purpose, which is to communicate the value system of capitalist society, is absolutely central to the radical argument. The Horrabins' claim is representative enough: the Labour Movement will not:

'demand a bias on the workers' side as either a necessary or a desirable qualification, but because it will know that the working-class view of history is the true one, and it will demand of its tutors, and for its students "the truth, the whole truth and nothing but the truth".'[19]

Such radical critics would be likely to reject, out of hand, statements like those which follow. They might claim that such statements are value laden, not objective, and cannot adequately be demonstrated as true or valid. Nor can it be assumed that the proponents of them are adequate judges in such matters.

'Our judgement of its cognitive richness has to be modified by our judgement of its objective worth as part of the furniture of reality, as something of which we can correctly say that, viewed quite on its own and apart from all consequences, its existence is in this or that degree objectively desirable, objectively good. Thus a painting by a Van Gogh or a Matisse, in its stark simplicity and austerity of tone and draughtsmanship, may lack the cognitive abundance offered by the work of some quite common-place artist of the late Baroque, but will nevertheless be judged, on grounds of pure aesthetic merit, to be a far more worthwhile object of contemplation by the serious student of art . . .'[20]

'Because the political theory of anarchism is of immense interest in its own right it deserves to be included in any course of social and political education, although—cut off as it is from many of the central questions by which Western political thinkers have been typically exercised—it has comparatively little to teach the student about social and political thought as a whole.'[21]

Radical critics would go on to claim that such cultural conservatism is detectable in most areas of learning and education. Thus, for example, traditional teaching of history or economics is not impartial, and is value-loaded. The radical criticism of such teaching is that history, as one example, is designed to perpetuate a mythology about the ordering of society, the glory of war, the dignity of imperial expansion, and the consolations of religion. It is a history of the powerful, in which the powerless play the part assigned to them. What actually were poor people doing while minor Court officials were gyrating about London? We have the voice of Elizabeth Fry: where are the voices of the prisoners? Where are the working class heroes? In the very early days of formal adult education these questions were raised. Mansbridge reported that:

'Professor Pollard, speaking to the Historical Association, said that working people were forcing historians to study the lives of ordinary people. Working men, he said, were not interested so directly in the literature and art of Greece as in how the common people lived.'[22]

This theme has been echoed in more recent criticism of the conventional historical package. In countries which have racial minorities, the latter have begun to observe that, apart from slave revolts, their place in history, or indeed in the culture of a nation is slight. American history is *not* just the history of the white race since the War of Independence, and British colonial behaviour may have been as reprehensible as that of the Spanish Conquistadors. Blacks have begun to articulate demands for history which reflects their

17

part in the moulding of their country, and of the world. Substantial groups, often majorities, are left out of account when history is relayed.

More generally, the historical purpose of education for subordinate groups in society is being questioned. The notion, that education serves a neutral function of equal benefit to those who dispense it, and to those who receive it, has been under particular attack. Nowhere is this more in evidence, at the present time, than in North America, with regard to education for black people.

A representative contribution to a major review of educational purpose in this respect is that by Donald Spivey.[23] He traces the rôle of education in perpetuating the social and political inferiority of the American blacks after the Civil War. During the period of reconstruction, the form and substance of Negro education was much debated, especially of course in the South. The overall policy soon became the establishment of 'industrial education', and organisations were soon set up for this purpose. The Superintendent of the Freedmen's Bureau, Armstrong, set up a famous establishment in Hampton, Virginia, on which his verdict was that:

'The South educated the blackman as a measure of self protection.'[24]

A former Confederate, and enthusiast for education in the post war South, J. L. M. Curry agreed, believing that order could be maintained 'not on brute force nor heavy armaments',[25] but by education. A white President of North Carolina College shared the popular view of what Blacks needed. As long after the War as 1900, he stated:

'His (the Negro's) colleges of law, of medicine, of theology, and of literature, science and art should be turned into schools for industrial training . . . The wasteful expenditure of money for negro literary education in the public schools of the South should be changed into profitable and useful training in industrial schools, shops and farms . . .'[26]

Nor, it is interesting to observe, were such ideas confined to Confederate whites. Booker T. Washington, the Black Principal of Tuskegee Institute wrote:

'Negro labour would never become excited by impossible ambition unless the spirit of unrest were stirred within him by education for which he was unfitted.'[27]

It is scarcely remarkable, given the frankness of such observations, that minorities have begun to question the social neutrality of education, to detect a social purpose which shapes the substance of that education, and to insist, for the sake of truth, that these be acknowledged.

Just as blacks have challenged conventional claims about the objective and rational nature of educational activity, so have women. The tradition of challenge from women is older, but in essence, it is the same. It is a rejection of the impartiality of education, and an insistence that education is designed to maintain the balance of power. This is the view of radical black writers, and of women who attack education as one of a number of male-dominated institutions.

Mary Wollstonecraft was an early critic, taking as a particular target Rousseau's ideas on education. In *Emile* Sophy is told:

'Emile, in becoming your husband, is becoming your master, and claims your obedience. Such is the order of nature.'[28]

It is hardly surprising that Wollstonecraft described Rousseau's ideas on women's education (and, by extension, their place in society) as 'one of Rousseau's wild chimeras'.[29]

The challenging feature of her criticism is that it turns Rousseau from being a popular example of revolutionary educational thought into a reactionary, leaving out of account a majority of the human race. This, of course, is the principal contribution of feminism to

18

societal analysis. It is to suggest that the bulk of those hailed as radicals, from Rousseau to Freire, do not pay sufficient attention to the position of women, in society or in education, in relation to men. The Marxist analysis, focusing as it does on relations between capital and labour, has barely begun to consider the theoretical and indeed practical implications of an examination of the power struggles between the sexes. Rousseau, it is felt, may be a hero to radical male educators, but his proposals for women are manifestly unpalatable.

Later, Virginia Woolf discussed the place of women in the body of knowledge which is transmitted through the educational process. Turning to history, she observes of women:
'One is held up by the scarcity of facts. One knows nothing detailed, nothing perfectly true and substantial about her. History scarcely mentions her. And I turned to Professor Trevelyan again to see what history meant to him . . . occasionally an individual woman is mentioned, an Elizabeth or a Mary; a queen or a great lady. But by no possible means could middle class women with nothing but brains and character at their command have taken part in any one of the great movements which, brought together, constitute the historian's view of the past.'[30]

This critical theme is developed by Hannah Gavron in respect of the education system generally. Her complaint is that it is a system which is designed for males, and females must manage as best they can:
'an educational system that treats little boys and little girls very much alike. This is not because the educational system has been altered in spirit, but because girls have simply been absorbed into it. Our system of education was designed for boys, and it has been assumed that girls fit in well enough.'[31]
It may be argued that the creation of the system is not so much assumed, as carefully studied and worked out.

Another emphasis once again of this theme is on the perpetuation of sexism through education. This, it is claimed, is achieved through the curriculum in both manifest and 'hidden' forms. A girl, for example, is expected to take 'feminine' subjects, such as needlework. But the pattern is even more sinister since the teaching is designed to get her to use her subject to reinforce her feminine rôle (subordinate, naturally,) in a male-dominated society. There is little need for our purpose to elaborate on these conclusions, since they are difficult to deny.[32] Ultimately, the dispute is about the rôle of women in society. If it is expected that their rôle is to be subordinate, then arguably the education system works perfectly well. The monopoly of male judgement in education, from Rousseau on, has led, until recently, to little real challenge. So that an eminent educator like John Newsom could say, presumably without a great deal of likelihood of contradiction:
'The future of women's education lies not in attempting to iron out their differences from men, to reduce them to neuters, but to teach girls how to grow into women and to re-learn the graces which so many have forgotten in the past thirty years.'[33]
This is a very clear illustration of the expectation that education is very much concerned with rôle preparation.

Kate Millett is just one example of a modern writer who is heir to this slim tradition which has been described, which challenges the notion of 'radical' when it is applied, and confined, to a male-dominated world. In a very erudite analysis of sexist culture she contrasts Ruskin and Mill in particular, and she demonstrates how the former, regarded as an educational hero by tradition, spells out clearly the rôle of education as a subjugator of women:
'A man ought to know any language or science he learns, thoroughly: while a woman ought to know the same language or science only so far as may enable

her to sympathize in her husband's pleasures, and in those of his best friends.'[34]

The rôle of what is called, in some ways unsatisfactorily, the 'feminist movement', in undermining traditional educational assumptions, has still not been properly understood. Nor has the educational system's means of neutralising it.

Systems, whether social or more specifically educational, can do this in a number of ways. In adult education, the most antique, and best tried, of these is to perpetuate the sexism of the schools. That is to allege that women need, and want, different kinds of courses. This leads, naturally, to the provision of courses which are manifestly relevant to the classical rôle of women—cookery, needlework, and so on. The question raised by feminists is to do with the relationship of such provision with the rôle of women in society. The answer, they typically claim, is clear.

In more recent years, adult educators have engaged in a number of strategies designed, as the more cynical might consider, to placate this radical spirit. One of the more conspicuous of these is the establishment of classes, or courses, *especially* for women. At first sight it would appear that the deflection of resources to such an end goes some way to proving the power of the feminist case. But it is arguable that the provision of such classes, which, empirical observation might conclude, affect only middle class housewives, does little to advance equality. Indeed, it may be that such provision heightens the eminence of men, and diminishes the validity of woman's claim to be equal.

The adult educator, in the real world, is likely to respond to such debates with the observation that the majority of adult educational courses are concerned with practical skills, which cannot have political, racist, or sexual overtones or intent. What conceivable relationship can there be between the ordinary adult educational classes and political structures? The simple answer is that there is indeed such a thing as a non-political dressmaking class. The radical critic would want the question broadened: Why is it that practical classes form such a large proportion of adult educational provision? Presumably because the demand is present. When this is examined, the political element, in its broadest sense, can be detected. The stimulation of the demand, the willingness to fulfil one demand and not another, are consequences of political decisions, made by people whose business is making decisions, which is to say the people with power. The reason why, for example, local authorities in Britain mount programmes of activity which are substantially practical and physical now becomes clear. It is because such activities are morally bland, and politically neutral. They pose no threat to existing assumptions, and insofar as they satisfy emotional need, they siphon off discontent. This in turn accounts for the turgidity of much discussion in conferences of adult educators. Classes become a placebo, remote from controversy, and the organisers resort to discussions of numbers attending, and the level of fees to be charged.

The harmlessness of adult education can be gauged from the way in which, when curbs are put upon educational expenditure, it is adult education which is regarded as elastic. In Britain, local educational authority provision for adult education, which is very slight compared with school expenditure, tends to be the first casualty in any public manifestation of reduced expenditure. This is because, it is argued, such classes are a luxury, and are not part of any seriously integrated provision. The importance of a university, more stable commitment, therefore becomes critical.

Furthermore, because the rationale behind decision making is not susceptible to public scrutiny or debate, a community is left with a *fait accompli* which cannot be challenged. That is to say, the decisions as to why a given programme of courses is mounted seem to be self evident. What is more difficult to discover is why certain options have been rejected, or more generally, what the options are, or might have been. This is, in part, a commentary on the naiveté of research in education, especially adult education.

Such criticism is a consequence of a belief in the manifestly indoctrinating rôle of traditional education. Such a rôle is political and anti-intellectual, and must be countered. It should be the duty of the adult educator to conduct a genuine search for truth which will lay bare the distortion which masquerades as impartiality and objectivity. Society should no longer accept the boundaries laid down for them, within which education takes place. The teacher should show that capitalism is not inexorable, delineating limits which are unassailable. A first step should be the challenge to those limits. 'In plain language', the Horrabins wrote, 'working class education must aim at the ending of Capitalism, and the building of a new social order.'[35] The task of education should be to change society: its success or failure should be measured accordingly.

In some ways radical writers blame universities most of all, for failing in such a task. The university manufactures a myth that it is a community of scholars pursuing truth, when in fact its main aim is to maintain the *status quo*, and anyone who doubts this could usefully note how universities, whose members are often so critical of the conservatism of others, have coped with dissent in recent years. Little else can be expected from institutions which rely so much on financial support from governments and powerful people.[36] The radical is not therefore surprised, as Millar remarks, that 'the average professor today is anti working class in outlook'.[37]

This view of universities as a good deal less radical, much more conservative, and less preoccupied with truth, than those working in them believe, is commonly found in radical writing. The universities, the argument runs, are especially to be condemned since they project an image alleging objectivity and a rationality which is their special preserve. In fact, however, this image masks the truth, which is that universities support whatever political system surrounds them. Reimer's is a representative view:

'Galbraith even argues that the academic community is one of our main hopes of escaping the worst implications of the new industrial state. The evidence does not support him. There is no major issue—war, pollution, exploitation, racism—on which the academic community, as such, has a discernible stand. There are intelligent courageous men in schools and universities, as there are elsewhere, but they receive no effective support from their institutions. In the exceptional case when an institution has shielded an unpopular dissident, it has also muffled his voice. The worst causes, on the other hand, have had no difficulty in recruiting academics to their support while institutions of learning have entered into contracts with all kinds of other institutions for all kinds of purposes.'[38]

So far the discussion has been about political boundaries and assumptions, and the views of people who see adult education as a tool which should be used to destroy those boundaries. A society is also stabilised by other assumptions and values which appear at first sight, and in conventional thinking, to have little to do with politics. One set of values, important for stability, and transmitted like other values, surrounds culture. The conventional view of culture, in the artistic sense, is that, for instance, certain kinds of literature are good, and other kinds are poor: that some music is aesthetically excellent, and some appals. This judgement has nothing to do with 'politics', since judgement about what is beautiful or ugly transcends the crude egocentricity of the political actors.

One of the great shocks for those holding such views in recent years has been the demand for 'relevance' in the arts. The responses to such demands have been, variously, denial, bewilderment and anger. Those who have an interest, often a central interest, in the purveying of culture may perhaps be forgiven for finding such an assault on traditional frameworks difficult to tolerate. There is much in the 'Black Papers' on education which reflects this. The 'Papers' go further. Much of what was written in those publications was sane and reasoned. But how is it possible to bring rational argument (so much vaunted) to bear when one of the articles reads:

'The word to be on the alert for, in all discussions of the direction in which syllabuses should be reformed, is "relevance"—to the needs of society, to a developed industrial society, to a bourgeois capitalist society, to the needs of the student, to the interests of the student. The student who is himself looking for relevance is looking for vocational training, a harmless desire in itself, though anti academic and therefore not to be indulged at a university: the teacher who wants to impart it is an enemy of culture. To extend the glossary a little: "challenging" or "exciting" courses of study are those in which a non subject or two, like sociology, social psychology, etc., is thrown to alleviate the burden of concentrating on a real subject.'[39]

Another writer expresses a common objection to innovation and change:

'The great god Mediocrity is always willing to look after his own. If you are not good enough for university and have to put up with a college of education, perhaps a B.Ed. may come your way, or you may find a technical college to give you a C.N.A.A. degree—and, failing all this, there will soon be the Open University. I still prefer Oxford and Cambridge, no matter how exotic the combination of the alphabet that is offered.'[40]

Those who attack the way in which culture is used to maintain stability claim, like those who are dissatisfied with the emphases of history, that life, as revealed and interpreted by the arts, does not square with the facts. The arts reflect a society inaccurately, and the resultant distortion is not a result of artistic exploration, but rather a deliberate attempt to pass on and perpetuate mythologies about society.

Such a belief gives new meaning to culture at all levels. The British film, especially the Comedy, on the whole depicts the upper class Englishman as patriotic without being chauvinistic, as inarticulate yet lovable, idiosyncratic but incapable of annoying, born to command yet devoid of snobbery. The working class man, on the other hand, is proud but dutiful, brave when given the right leadership, also inarticulate but laughable, and possessed of a sound sense which tells him that his best interests and those of his betters are identical. The radical critic will explain the indifference of poorer and powerless people to the interminable moralising of prigs in the Victorian novel, the myth making about soldier heroes, and the historic unreliability of non-powerful groups, as an awareness that 'culture' is awash with social commitment, and its transmission is a political act.

This notion of what has come to be called, variously, cultural imperialism, or invasion, takes the concept of radicalism a good deal beyond the narrow Marxist definitions, centred as they are around the capitalist phenomenon. Since this political aspect of 'culture' is so crucial to an understanding of some modern discussion of education, it is necessary now to look, in detail, at an example of radical adult education at work. The example is the Danish Folk High School Movement, the history of which is an almost perfect example of the interlocking relationship of politics and culture. A consideration of that history will further understanding of the meaning of radicalism, in adult education especially. In addition, the Danish Folk High School Movement is easily the most interesting part of the history of adult education.

REFERENCES

1.   R. Barrow, *Radical Education*, Martin Robertson, 1978, p. 1.

2.   In his Introduction Barrow develops an interesting, if hostile, set of common denominators which link radical educators.

3.   J. P. M. Millar, *The Trained Mind: Trained for What?*, National Council of Labour Colleges, n.d., circa 1927, p. 4.

4. 'Ivan the Fool', *Fellowship*, Vol. IV, No. 8, March 1918, ed. F. Sinclaire; reprinted in A. Wesson (ed.), *Basic Readings in Australian Adult Education*, Melbourne, Council of Adult Education, 1971.

5. Millar, op. cit., p. 7.

6. 'Ivan the Fool', op. cit.

7. Ibid.

8. Ibid.

9. E. Reimer, *School is Dead*, Penguin, 1971, p. 14.

10. Ibid., p. 138.

11. 'Ivan the Fool', op. cit.

12. I. Illich, *Deschooling Society*, Calder and Boyars, 1971, p. 24.

13. B. Jennings, 'Revolting Students—the Ruskin College dispute 1908-9', *Studies in Adult Education*, Vol. 9, No. 1, April 1977, p. 4.

14. Reimer, op. cit., p. 137.

15. Ibid., p. 138.

16. M. Sarup, *Marxism and Education*, Routledge and Kegan Paul, 1978, p. 51.

17. J. F. and W. Horrabin, *Working Class Education*, Labour Publishing Company, 1924, p. 71 (quoting J. H. Robinson, *The New History*, p. 133).

18. Ibid.

19. Ibid., p. 68.

20. R. W. K. Paterson, *Values, Education and the Adult*, Routledge and Kegan Paul, 1979, p. 88.

21. Ibid., p. 95.

22. A. Mansbridge, *The Kingdom of the Mind*, Meridian Press 1946 (originally published by E. M. Dent 1944), pp. 27-28.

23. Donald Spivey, *Schooling for the New Slavery: Black Industrial Education 1868-1915*, Greenwood Press, 1978.

24. Ibid., p. 35.

25. Ibid., p. 79.

26. Ibid., pp. 87-88 (quoting *Proceedings of the Southern Education Association*, Richmond, Virginia, December 1900, p. 116).

27. Ibid., p. 71 (quoting 'The Awakening of the Negro', *Atlantic Monthly* 78, 1896, pp. 327-8).

28. J. J. Rousseau, *Emile*, trans. B. Foxley, Dent (Everyman), 1948, p. 360.

29. M. Wollstonecraft, *Vindication of the Rights of Women*, 1792, p. 124.

30. Virginia Woolf, *A Room of One's Own*, Hogarth Press, 1949, p. 67.

31. Hannah Gavron, *The Captive Wife*, Routledge and Kegan Paul, 1966, p. 144.

32. For an analysis of this question *see* R. Deem, *Women and Schooling*, Routledge and Kegan Paul, 1978.

33. J. Newsom, *The Education of Girls*, Faber and Faber, 1948, p. 109.

34. Kate Millett, *Sexual Politics*, Hart-Davis, 1971, p. 97 (quoting Ruskin, *'Of Queen's Gardens'*, in *Sesame and Lilies*, p. 153).

35. J. F. and W. Horrabin, op. cit., p. 115.

36. Millar, op. cit., p. 5. For a development of this criticism *see* C. Wright Mills, *The Sociological Imagination*, Oxford University Press, 1959.

37. Millar, op. cit., p. 5.

38. Reimer, op. cit., pp. 147-8.

39. Kingsley Amis, *'Pernicious Participation'* in *'Fight for Education: a Black Paper'*, ed. C. B. Cox and A. E. Dyson, The Critical Quarterly Society, 1969, p. 10.

40. Arthur Pollard *'O and A Level: Keeping Up the Standards'*, in C. B. Cox and A. E. Dyson (eds.), *Black Paper Two: the Crisis in Education*, The Critical Quarterly Society n.d. 1970?

Chapter 3
Radicalism in Practice:
The Example of the Danish Folk High School

So far in this book the term 'radical' has been associated, substantially, with familiar, and conventional, political concepts. In particular the discussion has drawn upon examples of Marxist perceptions of capitalist societies. But radicalism, in the sense of an assault on social institutions and assumptions has wider meanings. An attack may be made on other elements in the Marxist 'superstructure' which could result in major social change, while leaving economic relationships intact. One such element is culture in all its aspects. Radical critics have always recognised the existence of 'cultural imperialism' and pointed out that it can be used to maintain undesirable social stagnancy. It can precede, accompany, or consolidate imperialism. Resistance to attempts to introduce alien cultures has increasingly been a focal point of radical thought and action. Perhaps the most remarkable, and successful, example of radical resistance to cultural imperialism is the Danish Folk High School Movement.

At the present time there are about 80 Folk High Schools in Denmark.[1] Each year about 9000 people attend, the majority of whom are under 25. Although there are some short courses of about a week, the bulk of the courses last between four and six months. The courses are liberal, non-vocational, involve no examinations or awards, and sometimes specialise in, for example, gymnastics. One absolutely crucial feature of the courses is that they are residential.

Each school is self-governing, but receives Government aid, and is subject to State inspection. Historically, the people who attend have been mainly from rural backgrounds. As the proportion of people working in agriculture has decreased, change in the balance has been reflected in High School attendance.

The Folk High School is a very good example of the fact that any adult educational institution or endeavour is the product of a particular social, geographical, and historical configuration. This is why attempts to transplant certain forms of adult education from one country to another are generally unsuccessful. The Folk High School, in precisely the form in which it developed in Denmark, is unique.

To understand its creation, and evolution, as a radical educational force, it is necessary to discuss the history of Denmark in the nineteenth century. It was out of the turmoil in which Denmark found itself after the Napoleonic Wars that the Schools arose. They were to become, in the view of Sir Richard Livingstone, 'the only great successful experiment in educating the masses of a nation'.[2]

The effect of the Napoleonic Wars on Denmark was calamitous. The country had been obliged to support the French, and one of the consequences of that support was that Norway was lost to Denmark. In addition, the country which had been a major maritime nation had lost its navy. The late eighteenth century initiative to reform Danish society, expressing itself for example in the abolition of serfdom, lost momentum. Agriculture, which was the backbone of the economy, was in a critical condition, and by 1815, the country faced bankruptcy. Despite such adversities, one remarkable reform took place, although not much discussed by historians of European education: in 1814, education was made compulsory for children between the ages of seven and fourteen.

Furthermore, in the first half of the century Denmark began to move from being an absolute monarchy to a liberal democracy, mainly because of revolutionary events elsewhere in Europe. Until 1831 the King's power was total, although at the end of the eighteenth and at the beginning of the nineteenth centuries, this power was used to introduce several liberalising measures. But with the ferment of ideas coming out of the Enlightenment, and the French Revolution and the Wars, it became clear that such power, however benevolent, could not persist.

In part because of pressures generated by the French Revolution of 1830, the King introduced a system of advisory councils. Now, for the first time, farmers were able to contribute to discussion about the government of the country. In June 1849, a democratic constitution was proclaimed. This growth of democracy was associated with the development of the Schools. When power began to be shared, certain key people, notably Grundtvig, were apprehensive lest devolution might be mishandled by newly enfranchised groups. It was felt that they should be 'educated' to use their new freedom wisely. This is a familiar theme in the history of adult education, and is found, for example, in the early history of the Workers' Educational Association in England.

Also in the 1840s there began a conflict which was to dominate the subsequent history of Denmark, and was the main *raison d'être* of the Folk High Schools. Germany was becoming increasingly strong and belligerent, and began to turn attention to the dispute over Schleswig—(Danish Slesvig) Holstein. The upheavals of 1848 had an effect in that region, when pro-German members of the population unsuccessfully rebelled against Danish rule.

By the 1860s, Bismark was in power, and in 1864 war broke out between Denmark and Prussia and Austria. For Denmark the results were disastrous. In February 1864, the Danish army was driven back from its ancient fortification in the south called *Dannevirke*, and in April the redoubts at another famous fortification, the *Dybbøl* collapsed. The outcome of the war was that Denmark lost $\frac{2}{5}$ths of her land and $\frac{1}{3}$rd of her population, many of whom, it must be conceded, were German speaking. Within the lifetime of many Danes the country had experienced little more than calamities. The view was soon expressed after 1864 that the liberalising 1849 constitution was, in some way, responsible for the disaster. The consequence was a revised constitution in 1866 which limited the franchise to a privileged segment of the population.

Out of this period, with the accompanying intellectual development and debate, came a Danish national hero, whose role in the creation of the Folk High School must now be considered: Nikolaj Severin Frederick Grundtvig (1783-1872). It is generally agreed that he was the intellectual source of the methods, aims, and assumptions of the Schools. He was a clergyman, scholar of Old Norse and Old English, philosopher and poet.[3] It was in connection with his studies that the King agreed to support a request to go to England to study Anglo-Saxon manuscripts. Grundtvig stayed in England from 1829-1831, and that period was of the greatest significance in his intellectual development and ultimately on the Folk High School.

One result of his experience at Oxford and Cambridge was that he became an advocate of residential adult education. The residential component of the Folk High School is the linchpin. It is commonly claimed that there is a direct link between the experience of living together in the Schools and the spirit of collaboration which facilitated the Co-operative movement, which is so important in Denmark.

The second major effect of his experience in England was the development of a vision of how Norse history and mythology could be channelled into Danish adult education. This was to be the cornerstone of the High School curriculum. But he did not, as radical educators sometimes do, 'see the past as a Golden Age',[4] For him the past was to be used to re-establish Danish pride. Students would see in history answers to contemporary problems.

History meant *Danish* or, more generally, Nordic history. The narrow, classical, book-dominated education, which was general in Danish schools, was alien. And because it was alien it could not encourage the feeling of being proud of being a Dane, which Grundtvig believed was so desirable. There was, however, a more sinister threat to Denmark than the cultural assumptions of classical writers, and this threat was coming from Germany.

This is a matter which will be discussed later, but it is necessary to consider Grundtvig's views on Germany since, like all his views, these were important in the developing educational strategy in the Schools. The tension between universal values and the encouragement to nationalism is to be expected in a writer who was both a Christian and a nineteenth century Dane. Furthermore, like all intellectual and prolific writers, he is not invariably consistent in his statements. He seems to have believed that *Folkeaanden* or 'national spirit'[5] was essential if a society was to survive, but that national pride need not express itself in negative or destructive attitudes to other peoples. The distinctions, if they can exist in reality between a passive and an aggressive nationalism, are very obscure. The truth is that the Folk High Schools were unequivocally anti-German. Nor is there much doubt about Grundtvig's opinion of his neighbour:

'Even if I were 90 years old, I should have myself carried out of a country in which a German or a Russian ruled.'[6]

'Denmark is like a beautiful young girl who is molested by a German warrior.'[7]

'Even the tyranny France practised under Napoleon in Europe would be only a bagatelle compared with that of . . . Germany under its God of War, who would certainly make his presence felt. For the German earnestness and thoroughness would in this direction be ten times more oppressive than the French volatility and superficiality, and we poor Danes, who have difficulty enough in defending our own characteristics against a Germany of small states, would easily be completely swallowed by a united one.'[8]

When Danes, including some who write about the High Schools, discuss the anti-German feelings which dominate Danish history, they sometimes understate them. This is partly because the pacifist movement in this century found sympathisers amongst important members of the High School movement, and partly because of a change in relationship between the two countries in recent years. In any case, the Schools have always considered themselves Christian, or Humanist, or in some other way to stand for general, universal, principles of friendship. Crude anti-German propaganda is clearly not consonant with such principles, and this seems to present some Danes with a considerable intellectual difficulty. That anti-German feeling *was* encouraged by the High Schools is beyond dispute, even if it was governments, and not the German people, who were the objects of that feeling.

Grundtvig contributed to the radical task of the emerging Schools not only by making the development of national spirit the main aim, but by encouraging innovation in educational methodology to that end. Barrow points out an interesting feature of radical educators in his claim that they are 'suspicious of book learning'[9] and this is certainly true of Grundtvig. He was fond of contrasting the 'living' spoken word with the 'dead' written word.[10] The rote learning of his day he regarded as very 'dead' indeed, and must be replaced by learning through talking. The spoken word would enable students to understand their heritage, to share their experiences, and, through verbal explanation and exploration, give them some appreciation of what was great in past and present. In this advocacy of the spoken word he was a good deal ahead of what has become common educational practice.

The use of the living word would encourage not only an intellectual appreciation of Denmark, but would excite feeling in the students. He seems to have felt that, without emotional activity in the learning process, students would not develop into complete people. The connection between language, nationalism, and emotion is a constant theme in his writings.

'A people are tied first and last by the language, the native tongue, the ties of the heart which embrace high and low, the word of strength which lives in the mouth of the people.'[11]

Grundtvig, being a Christian minister in the nineteenth century, believed his objectives and methods were entirely consonant with Christian teaching. He envisaged a situation when a person establishes his identity and dignity through education, and from there becomes a Christian. In this association of education and Christianity there are parallels with Cardinal Newman's beliefs. The two met, incidentally.

Grundtvig never opened a Folk High School, although he had a vision of a great institution in a town called Sorø. A school was named after him in 1856 in his lifetime at Marielyst. The Grundtvig Folk High School was subsequently moved and is now at Fredericksborg in North Zealand.

The Folk High School Movement actually began in North Slesvig, against a background, as has been pointed out, of encroaching German culture. In the early 1840s in that district, the language used in secondary education, in the law courts, and in the churches, was German. It was precisely to arrest and reverse this situation that Christian Flor established the first Folk High School at Rødding in 1844. Its task was to act 'as a spiritual fortification against the Germans'.[12] This objective was stressed in the opening speech of the first principal, Johan Wegener.[13]

His speech lamented the passing of Denmark's glory. Wegener related how territory had been lost, and how a considerable danger was at hand—a quarter of Denmark was in danger of being 'Germanised'. Rødding High School was going to prevent this. The new Principal, however, had a rather narrow view of 'political'. Although he was advancing what can only be described as political aims, he rejected 'speaking politics to uneducated young persons (and) filling their brains with political ideas'. Upon reflection, he pointed out that 'if the endeavour to thwart all attempts to suppress and debase our mother tongue were to be called political', then politics would be involved.

Nevertheless, he discouraged any negative assessment of the Germans. They were 'a great and fine nation' and because of kinship Danes ought to 'make this people our closest friends' . . . 'Love of one's country is not tantamount to hatred of one's enemies'. It should be remembered that he was speaking some twenty years before the 1864 disaster. When he left the School, Wegener, in his final speech, was violently political. He described how he had told the students that:

'it was up to them whether all that they saw and heard was to be the last agony of a dying nation, or an awakening to renewed life . . . I saw courage in despair shining from their eyes.'[14]

As a result of the 1864 War, South Jutland and Rødding became German territory. A new Folk High School was opened in Askov, a short distance north of the new border. The population in the annexed area fell, in part because Danes wished to avoid Prussian military service. Since the teaching of Danish was forbidden, Danes had to develop an alternative system of education. As soon as Danish children finished their German education, they attended continuation schools in Denmark, and in increasing numbers went to the Folk High Schools.[15] Askov in particular became a focus of resistance, and the Schools in general became:

'the workshop from which more and more people of Slesvig obtained their weapons for the fight for Danish culture.'[16]

A German inhabitant of the area agreed, commenting that:
> 'Our youth leave the Danish Folk High School and return home with the unshakeable conviction that they obey the German authority only because it has the power, and not because they feel a sense of moral obligation towards their foreign rulers,'[17]

In fact the battle against the Germans was to be fought, after 1864, not with weapons but with education:
> '1864 transformed the Grundtvigian High Schools into strongholds of Danish civilisation—walls more durable than those of Dannevirke and Dybbøl.'[18]

Many Danes, some of whom were eminent, gave up careers to work in the High Schools after 1864, to help with the building of these intellectual defences.[19]

Mention must be made of the most eminent of the practitioners of the Folk High School men, Christen Kold (1816-1870). Kold ranks second to Grundtvig in the hagiography of Danish national educational heroes. His father was a shoemaker, and the son had a varied life, including a period as a servant, and as a bookbinder, in Syria. When he returned to Denmark, after consulting Grundtvig, he opened a school at Ryslinge in 1850. Kold shared Grundtvig's views almost totally, and put many of his principles into practice. They disagreed about the ideal age for students, Kold believing that 15 was the best and Grundtvig 18. Eventually, as a result of experience, Kold conceded that Grundtvig was right. The most significant point of agreement was their rejection of the domination of books in education, and their wish to infuse practice with 'living' language. Kold's especial contribution was to establish the connection between the Folk High School and rural life. Because of his humble background and his simple style of life he was able to communicate with the Danish peasantry in a way which was quite outside the experience of more traditional educational institutions such as the universities.

The Danish Folk High School system has grown steadily since the pioneers opened the first institutions. Any attempt to assess their impact presents formidable methodological problems, since there has been little systematic attempt to evaluate adult education, especially in a historical context. It must address itself to the question as to the task which the system set itself, and how successful it was.

The central goal was to ensure the survival of Denmark as a cultural entity in the face of German cultural and military invasion. It seemed to observers in the nineteenth century that Denmark might follow other small nations into oblivion, or at least be forced to decline into a state of cultural subservience. Today it is a strong, independent society with an impressive liberal tradition. But how far that is due to German military setbacks, or to the work of the schools, is difficult to assess. There is little doubt, however, that especially after 1864, they acted as a focal point for national aspirations, more particularly in respect of lost territory.

To the High School leaders after 1864 'the ultimate object was South Jutland's restoration to Denmark'.[20] That objective was central until the outbreak of war in 1914, and 'from the High Schools we recruited the future leaders in the national struggle south of the frontier'.[21] South Jutlanders who were members of the German Reichstag and of the Prussian Diet before 1914 were former High School students, and the four North Slesvig delegates sent to the 1919 Peace Conference to negotiate reunion were all ex-Schoolmen.[22] The outcome was that South Jutland was returned to Denmark, and in 1920 that symbol of resistance, Rødding Folk High School, re-opened.

The Peace Conference did not placate German territorial ambitions, and in April 1940, Denmark was occupied. The rôle of the Schools during that occupation is a highly controversial matter. They continued to function and were able 'to continue their cultural struggle against Nazi barbarism, and their eloquent defence of Danish democracy'.[23] Critics have claimed that they were not sufficiently active, and it has been conceded that 'by and large the High School men were not to be found on the barricades, fighting on by means of machine-guns and sabotage'.[24] A Secretary-General of O.E.C.D., Thorkil Kristensen, alleged that:

> 'The friends of the High School have to admit that it has not, in the inter-war years, been the stimulus they had hoped for, and which we so badly needed. Further, in the national regeneration, which was not lacking under German oppression, the High School and the farmer class (which supplied most of its students) were not in the front rank.'[25]

There was, as elsewhere in Europe, a certain amount of support amongst Danes for Nazi politics. But the main reason for this lack of aggression was the growth of pacifism in the 1920s and 1930s, which influenced some of the Schools. This influence expressed itself in a number of ways, from the elimination of blatantly martial, patriotic songs from the High School song book[26] to the establishment of the International People's College at Elsinore in 1921. This College has sought to apply the philosophy of the Folk High Schools to the international search for peace and understanding. Nevertheless, defenders of the Schools point to what they construe as significant actions, such as the condemnation of Nazi policies at a national Folk High School convention in 1934.

In 1945 it seemed as though the classical nationalism of the Schools would be resurrected, when there was agitation for the removal of the border to the south, in order that South Slesvig, which had been lost in 1864, could be returned to Denmark. The Danish government refused to support this ambition, and the movement faded away. It is unlikely that boundary disputes will act as a focus for High School effort in the foreseeable future, especially since Denmark and Germany are partners in the European Economic Community.

Because of the original task of the Schools, the changes in attitudes to war and nationalism after 1918 were of great significance to the High School system. It is probable that, with the rejection of the unequivocal nationalism of the pre-1914 era, the Schools lost some of their direction. Instead of maintaining the old, apparently anachronistic goal, the movement now developed more general, yet socially purposeful aims. Broadly, these were directed at improving Danish society, and contributing to international understanding. It is Folk High School success in these areas that has been stressed by more recent commentators.

One claim which is made for success in the field of radicalism is the part the Schools played in resisting political reaction following the 1864 crisis. Grundtvig himself protested to the Parliament, and to the King, over the restriction of the franchise in 1866.[27] This resistance of attempts to halt the development of a democracy was recognised by the Conservative elements. The Schools, during the last part of the nineteenth century, were regarded with suspicion, and were variously accused of contributing to 'naive nationalistic complacency',[28] of being vague, and of not engaging in enough practical work.

Many such complaints are commonly made against educators who deviate from the views held by traditionalists as to what educational aims should be. In Denmark, as happens elsewhere, this suspicion was translated into action by discrimination against Schools which the government found especially offensive. Askov, for example, at one period had its grant withdrawn. By 1892, political reaction was sufficiently contained to allow the passing of an important Act, which ensured that the Schools would receive unconditional aid.

More specific claims are made about the effectiveness of the High Schools than this generalised contribution to the development of a liberal democracy. It is also alleged that the success of Danish farming and the considerable success of the Co-operative Movement both owe a great deal to the work of the Schools. Naturally, it is conceded that other factors played a part. The repeal of the Corn Laws in England in 1846, for instance, opened up new markets for Danish produce. Nevertheless, supporters of the Schools would claim that the farmers who watched the battles fought by the School against reactionary governments followed their example when they had to choose between domination by big business and independence through co-operation. The connections are set out in an especially convinced statement by a Director of the Co-operative Movement, Anders Nielsen:

'It (the High School) has filled in and levelled the cleavages in society and thereby paved the way for common endeavour. It has sent students out into life with an increased love for the country and its achievements, riper and more thoughtful, more perceptive to life's teaching, and therefore better equipped to understand and make their way . . . not only the co-operative movements but the cultural position of Danish farmers as a whole rests on this foundation.'

'When we consider the social importance of the co-operative movement and its economic contribution to the national development, we must acknowledge with gratitude the great religious and educational leaders Grundtvig and Kold and their many co-workers and followers who have called forth a higher culture and a feeling of solidarity among the people, and who have also taught the people to think and use their powers so that not only the individual but the whole community is benefited.'[29]

At the heart of both Danish farming and co-operation is the tradition of dialogue and communication of ideas which were the essence of the work in the Schools. All of which were cemented by the experience of living together, which in turn engendered mutual understanding. Sir Richard Livingstone, an enthusiastic advocate of residential education in England based on the Danish model, was in no doubt. The experience of residence in the Folk High Schools led to:

'this spirit which helped to make the Danish Co-operative Movement possible.'[30]

The result was that:

'Every Dane would agree that the impulse which gave inspiration and zest to national life and raised the country from bankruptcy to prosperity, came from the High School with its peculiar humanistic education.'[31]

Danish historians of the School system agree: 'Grundtvig's bust ought to be placed at the door of every Danish co-operative establishment.'[32] They generally quote the famous example of the ex High School student who reported that:

'it is in the spirit of the Nordic myths, as in youth I heard them from Schrøder's mouth at Askov, that I tilled my land.'[33]

These are bold claims. One rather more sober way of trying to evaluate the connections between the Schools and society might be to analyse the backgrounds and careers of ex-students. At the same time, some methodological device would have to be developed so that this experience at the Schools could be isolated as a factor. Such a considerable task is beyond the scope of this book. But from time to time, some interesting indicators are drawn up. For example, Jacob Appel was Minister of Education 1920-1924, during part of the time he was Principal of Askov 1906-1928.

J. T. Arnfred, his successor at Askov 1928-1956, was very prominent in the Co-operative Movement. Gammelgaard, the Principal of Roskilde was a member of the local committee of the Resistance during the Occupation.[34] 'A rough examination' in 1930 showed that of all the chairmen of the Co-operative Dairy Associations, 54% had attended Folk High Schools, 23% Agriculture Schools, and 2% Dairy Schools.[35]

Such figures are clearly inadequate for an attempt to prove conclusively the effectiveness of the School system, or to demonstrate that it was *the* important causal factor in Denmark's development. Research into all these matters has a long way to go to allow the validity of Rørdam's summary:

'The spiritual inspiration given by the High Schools to the young from the farms was converted to a spirit of practical enterprise. The High Schools must be given credit for the excellent quality of Danish butter, for the excellent organization of our agricultural production and exports, as well as for the share that Danish farmers have done in the work of Government, Parliament and local government.'[36]

Even allowing for the boldness of such claims, and the hagiography surrounding men like Grundtvig and Kold, there remains an impressive and general conviction in Denmark, and in Danish writing, that without the work of the High Schools, Denmark would not have developed as it has. This is a 'feeling', perhaps of the kind that Grundtvig wished to encourage amongst the people: the emotional commitment to their past which would lead to social integrity in the present. Perhaps it is an emotional attitude to the rôle of the High Schools, which would not be supported by intellectual analysis. It is certainly true that a rigorous appraisal is due. But such an inquiry must start with the fact that today Denmark is a small, independent nation, with an impressive tradition of liberalism. And that, one hundred years ago, it seemed probable that it would be destroyed by a weight of German military and cultural aggression.

There remains the question as to the future rôle of the Folk High Schools. With the change in international relationships, and the high level of democracy and national pride in modern Denmark, is there still a radical task? This is a question which will be discussed later.

REFERENCES

1. The standard text is Thomas Rørdam, *The Danish Folk High Schools*, Det Danske Selskab, 1965, rev. ed. 1980.

2. Richard W. Livingstone, *Future in Education*, C.U.P., 1941, p. 44.

3. There are many accounts of Grundtvig's life and work. *See* for example H. Koch, *Grundtvig*, Antioch, 1952.

4. R. Barrow, *Radical Education*, Martin Robertson, 1978, p. 2.

5. This translation is by P. Manniche (and an international group of writers), *Denmark: a Social Laboratory*, Pergamon, 1969, p. 96.

6. P. G. Lindhardt, *Grundtvig—an Introduction*, S.P.C.K., 1951, p. 58 (quoting *Danskeren I*, 1890, p. 214).

7. Ibid., p. 97 (quoting *Danskeren I*, p. 58).

8. Ibid., p. 58 (quoting *Mands Mind*, p. 376 ff.).

9. Barrow, op. cit., p. 2.

10. Manniche, op. cit., p. 96.

11. Lindhardt, op. cit., p. 95 (quoting *Vaerker in Udvalg* ved Georg Christensen og Hal Koch VIII, 1940).

12. H. Begtrup, H. Lund and P. Manniche, *The Folk High Schools of Denmark and the Development of a Farming Community*, O.U.P., 1929, p. 133.

13. An account is given in Rørdam, op. cit., pp. 46-7.

14. Ibid, p. 49.

15. Begtrup et al., op. cit., p. 71.

16. Ibid., p. 72.

17. Ibid.

18. Rørdam, op. cit., p. 67 (quoting *Højskolen Gennem 100 år* R. Skovmand, p. 45).

19. Manniche, op. cit., p. 106. *See also* Rørdam, op. cit., p. 88.

20. Rørdam, op. cit., p. 88.

21. Ibid.
22. Ibid. *See also* Begtrup et al., op. cit., p. 72.
23. Ibid., p. 98.
24. Ibid.
25. Ibid.
26. Ibid., p. 89.
27. Ibid., p. 69. Rørdam in CH. 5 discusses the post-1864 period in detail.
28. Ibid., p. 75.
29. Manniche, op. cit., p. 83.
30. R. W. Livingstone, 'The Danish People's High Schools: a Reply', *Adult Education*, Vol. XIV, No. 3, March 1942, pp. 109-110. The reply was to H. Morris, who was not convinced of the relevance of the system to Britain. *See* 'The Danish Folk High School Myth, *Adult Education*, Vol. XIV, No. 2, December 1941.
31. Ibid.
32. Begtrup et al., op. cit., p. 139.
33. Rørdam, op. cit., p. 151.
34. Ibid., p. 127.
35. Manniche, op. cit., p. 103 (quoting Begtrup et al., op. cit., p. 53).
36. Rørdam, op. cit., p. 151.

Chapter 4

After Success:
Adult Education in a Changed Society

The early radicals, as we have seen, proposed that conventional education in school, or in the evening class, was committed to the preservation of existing relationships, whether dominated by Capitalism, by German Imperialism or any other power. If a real quest for Truth were injected into the education of people, then those people would realise the crippling defects of existing systems, and would try to overthrow them. In Marxist ideology, the collapse of Capitalism would herald the era of Socialism. In Denmark, Germanism would be destroyed, although the events of the Second World War reminded Denmark how quickly it could re-appear. The arrival of victory and of the new society does pose an interesting problem. When the desired restructuring has taken place, what should the aim of adult education be?

This was not a question which was discussed by early radicals such as the Horrabins. From the standpoint of the early twentieth century observer, English Capitalism seemed well entrenched, and although there was a faith in the inevitability of its collapse, this seemed to many to be remote. All their energies were devoted to its overthrow, rather than with discussion about some hypothetical situation which would arise afterwards. It is also the case that classical Marxism is, itself, rather short of answers to questions about the Utopia where the state will, in the famous phrase, 'wither away'. Finally, earlier writers did not, of course, have access to the experience which we have at present, of observing adult education at practice in Socialist countries, which should, theoretically, have achieved the ideal aims of adult education as set out by the radicals. So, what *does* happen to adult education when its aim of ending Capitalism has been achieved, which result may, it need hardly be stressed, have little to do with education, and more to do with judicious manipulation of armies?

An analysis of the writing of adult educators, and indeed educators in general, from Eastern Europe or Cuba, reveals that the underlying assumptions are only slightly changed. Socialism is still Truth, and since education is concerned with the latter it is still linked to the former. The rôle of adult education now becomes the consolidation of the achievement. There is no need to work for a new order in society, but there is still a need to integrate people into it, especially since there is always a danger of domination by Capitalist forces, hostile to the new Socialist society. It is, of course, no longer appropriate to challenge boundaries, social, political or cultural, since in a sense there are none which are in conflict with people's wishes. The old boundaries were generated by the injustice of Capitalism. When Capitalism is ended, the constraints are removed. But unless people understand what has happened, these may re-appear. So the educator should set out to integrate and make firm the new society.

In the U.S.S.R., the first country to implement, allegedly, a Marxist régime, the value of education in the task of consolidation seems to have been appreciated. The revolutionary government began with mass literacy campaigns. The eradication of illiteracy is always popular as a goal with left wing revolutionary governments. In the U.S.S.R., this led to further education, with the aim that the people of central Asia, and other areas which, under the Tsars were extremely backward, would:

> 'utilise the benefits of contemporary education and raise themselves to the pinnacles of socialist culture.'[1]

The successes claimed by those involved in such mass adult education are considerable, and one is left wondering why the attempts to eradicate illiteracy in other parts of the world are notably less successful.

In India, for example, there are probably, at the present time, more people who are illiterate, than there were at the beginning of the century. In Cuba, on the other hand, it is claimed that in 1953, 23.6% of the population over the age of ten were illiterate. After the revolution, as a result of the 1961 National Literacy Campaign, illiteracy was reduced to 3.9%.[2] Assuming that such reports are at least substantially true, and there is little doubt in some cases that they are, not only is this the result of the deployment of substantial resources, but is a consequence of the successful motivation of the learners. What has been the driving force which has raised educational levels in some revolutionary countries? The generic theme is the wish to use education to develop a Socialist awareness.

The Cuban Ministry of Education offers the traditional explanation for the lack of interest on the part of the people:

'Because of its approach and content this teaching was dissociated from life and there was open divorce between theory and practice.'[3]

In place of this:

'Cuba is developing a new type of education aimed at the formation of a new type of man that the revolutionary process requires. This process is based on a specific morality and ideology determined chiefly by active participation of the people in the tasks set by the revolution.'[4]

Cuba's intention that 'education is aimed at the complete formation of man' is a constant theme in post revolutionary left wing writing. Lenin's reported view was:

'that it was part of education's job to help the masses to understand and grasp the significance and rôle of revolutionary changes.'[5]

As in Cuba, such a goal involved a radical change in the working of educational systems:

'From an instrument of class domination, the school became an instrument of profound social transformation.'[6]

The publications of other Socialist countries report the same patterns. Hungarian adult educators define their task as 'building up a socialist society'. The ultimate in that society will be 'the socialist man' who 'is consciously and actively engaged in building society according to the Marxist-Leninist programme of socialism and communism'.[7] This, in essence, is what all communist adult educators explain as their task.

Much of the discussion so far has been concerned with the Marxist critique of conventional education, and all the discussion about a post revolutionary situation has been about communist or quasi communist societies. What, if any, is the attitude and behaviour of politically extreme right wing governments to adult education? Fascist or neo Fascist governments do not usually base their educational policies on theories of any complexity. The extreme right wing group tends to regard education with suspicion and contempt. When there is a right wing revolution, therefore, the usual practice is to close down adult education facilities, rather than to use them. There have been rare exceptions, and it is worth mentioning one—Fascist Italy—since it provides an interesting comparison with communist societies. The most interesting fact which emerges is that, although the ideologies underlying political structures and organisations between, say, an Eastern European country and Fascist Italy are as different as it is possible to be, the common denominator is agreement about how education should be used in this new aim of consolidating Utopia.

At the end of the last century, there was established in Italy "La Società Umanitaria". By the 1920s it was providing a substantial amount of adult education but it was not, in Mussolini's words, producing 'man of few words, of cold courage, of tenacious industry, of blind discipline'.[8] But the Fascists did not close the institution. Instead, they changed its teaching, by infusing into that teaching the ideas of Fascism. The same happened in another institution, the Universita Popolare (the Popular University). Italians continued to attend them, but now there was an attempt:

> 'to diffuse among the people a healthy culture, to focus light upon the noble traditions and great glory of the Patria in history, letters, the arts and sciences.'[9]

Such an aim, in its emphasis on the glory of the long past and the decadence of the immediate past, is reminiscent of the Danish Folk High School, but devoid of its universal, liberalising, values. It is equally reminiscent of the work of socialist educators, except that the historical emphasis is different, in that different parts of historical evolution are stressed and utilized.

How readily an individual will accept the deployment of adult education as a force to integrate Utopian, final societies, or how far the prospect of such a rôle should silence radical criticism, depends, obviously enough, upon personal commitment. The critic of communist or fascist adult education may feel that new boundaries have been erected which look suspiciously like the old. Indeed, prohibition on challenging those boundaries may be even more rigid, since the new structures are based on carefully thought out political ideologies which, at the most extreme, have the same disadvantages as religious creeds. Both insist on certain assumptions being unquestioned before education can be tolerated. Both are substantially based on dogma, which is 'revealed', rather than demonstrated. Both are, therefore, anti-intellectual, and apprehensive of challenge. There are many examples of these new restrictions replacing the old. At the one extreme there are the writings of Solzhenitsyn and others who catalogue the depressing Philistinism of the New Order. On a more casual level there are the frequent newspaper reports, which cannot all be the product of conspiracies, of crude repression of intellectual debate. A typical report appeared in September 1974, which related how Soviet artists who staged an 'unofficial' abstract art show watched the authorities break it up, remove pictures and send people to detention for 'hooliganism'.[10]

Thus the critic of post revolutionary adult education tends to level the charge that the socialist or fascist educator (where he exists) is different from his capitalist counterpart only because he believes in the evident Truth of his assertions. It is in the Socialist and Fascist countries that it has become increasingly difficult to write a non 'political' novel, or to compose a non 'political' piece of music. Radicalism has won, it seems, and begins to look suspiciously like conservatism:

> 'The Soviet school of today leads the world in respect of range of instruction, the level of knowledge it imparts and the ideological and moral orientation of the education it provides.'[11]

Is this alleged achievement acceptable? Should the radical comply with the rôle now thrust upon him that he should integrate the Utopia? This problem has always posed theoretical difficulties for Marxists, since the static proposition of the socialist state seems so out of accord with the history of societies which seem constantly to begin to undermine a new order almost as soon as it is established. It is not appropriate to develop this argument here, only necessary to note that a new view of society as static-after-revolution leaves educators with unanswered questions, some very old and none new.

The Danish Folk High Schools may be discussed, once again, as a practical example. The schools had to ask themselves what their rôle should be when their initial radical task—rejecting Germanism, and developing a corporate national identity—was achieved. National pride is fostered most easily when it is threatened. When there is no threat, there is

35

a hollowness about educational exhortations to develop it. When it is manifestly present, then such exhortations are tiresome.

Since the schools are such remarkable institutions, and since the maturity of Danish society, at least to outsiders, seems to be one of the wonders of the modern world, it is to be expected that their current and future rôle should be discussed, once an historical episode was finished. One feeling expressed is that since the School Movement has achieved its aim, it will wither away. Paul Dam, a High School Principal, is reported to have said to UNESCO that:

'in 10-15 years, the Danish Folk High School will have ceased to exist.'[12]

To others, experienced in the System, there is still a great deal to do. Denmark, in common with many other countries, is witnessing a significant movement from the countryside to the town. Manniche suggests that:

'Folk High School teaching may prove to be of great value at a time when the agricultural community tends to be transformed into a manufacturing one, with the changed outlook this concurrently involves.'[13]

The movement retains, however, a number of characteristics which make the outlook rather promising. Three of the most important of these are the radical tradition, the independent administrative structure, and its non association with the technical and technological in education. The importance of the last of these is that the debates about increase or decrease of technological provision, with which many other bodies might become involved, have no relevance for the movement. The movement is, perhaps, the most uncompromising advocate of liberal education in the world.

Many of the Folk High Schools have, in fact, adapted to changes in the structure and culture of Danish society. The migration from country to town in the wake of industrialisation, which has been rapid since the Second World War, has been matched in some places by provision of courses for older age groups, and a broadening of the range of subjects offered. The self examination has, it is claimed, at least at one school, led to a basic questioning as to how the quintessential radicalism of the movement can be used to improve society. The German target is no more; can another be identified?

The new school at Kolding is an attempt to delineate one. The staff, it appears, are not satisfied, either with the lack of radicalism in many schools, or with the implication—that society is satisfactory. The aims of this new venture are as radical as ever, in that the purpose is to initiate social change. The objects have been described by one of the teachers, Jorgen Knudsen:

'To elucidate and discuss the conflicts and contradictions which govern society and human life;
To help to indicate alternative ideas and possibilities in the light of given conditions and trends of development;
And to promote a change in the conditions which distort and repress human life.'[14]

An interesting comment on the maturity of Danish society and the healthy state of liberal education is that the new school is built on land belonging to the local council, and that the money was raised from government grant, and from supporters, some of whom were principals and teachers at traditional schools.

This venture in a small Folk High School in Denmark is more significant than appears at first sight: it exemplifies a new radicalism. It has been noted that the Marxist proposition about the rôle of adult education, which seemed tenable before the socialist experience of the last fifty years, leaves unsolved the question as to the need for radical challenge to assumptions about education, and the direction any such challenge should take. There has developed, in recent years, a critical assessment of education, including adult education, and its function in society, which promises to break the stagnant grip of traditional radical theorising. Broadly, the proposition of the new critics is not that men are repressed solely by capitalism, and its tool education (although some are), but that modern man, peasant or townsman, is powerless, unhappy and alienated because of what modern, massive state institutions do to him.

The new radical critic—of society and of education—is not impressed by ingenious, complete, political solutions. Inheriting, and reflecting upon, the experience of almost every kind of permutation of government, he claims that the problem goes beyond the repression of any one political system. The problem is immanent in the nature of the modern state with its proliferation of political and organisational machines. If the modern state is to stay in its present form, then there will always be a need for constant critical examination of its institutions. There is no Utopia: there is only the need to correct the tendency to excess by the powerful.

Education in society is a popular target. The new critics challenge the assumptions underlying the ideology of this institution in several ways. Two are especially important here. The first is the dominance of technology and technical education. The second is the fact that expansion of education has been programmed not by the needs of society, but by the needs of those who work in education.

This is not to say that critics dismiss entirely the need for technical and technological training. What is of concern is the constant battle between the technical trainers and those who believe that a liberal education is essential. It is, perhaps, a universal, timeless struggle, which is part of the liberal educator's life. In a microcosmic, though real, form, this battle is fought, daily, in education establishments in Britain. The criticism of purely technical training such as that given to doctors, lawyers, chemists or motor mechanics is not that it makes them professionally competent, one hopes, but that they fail to understand many significant, and some vital, matters to do with living in society. They typically know little of art, or of literature, are conservative in approach and because of the professional circle in which they move, know little of the social problems which are debated at any time. This Philistinism is evidenced by the hostility teachers of technical subjects show towards the liberal components of an educational course.

There is another criticism which leads to the broader attack made by observers such as Illich. This is that much of the technical and technological expansion which is taking place throughout the world is merely the consequence of educators manipulating the situation. The shortage of science and technology students may indicate, as teachers of those subjects would insist, that the prospect of the hard work involved deflects students into easier courses. The critic would counter this by suggesting that students find technical courses dreary, and intellectually and emotionally unsatisfying. Further, the post course experience is coming to show, increasingly, that jobs in such narrow professional areas are difficult to find. In other words, education no longer serves society adjusting to needs (indeed those needs seem no longer to be recognised), but has become an institution whose task is to minister to the needs of the people who run it. This is becoming a familiar story which is a feature, not only of education, but of medicine, the Civil Service and other giant organisations which do not have to show a financial profit. All modern states proliferate their educational institutions and compete for precedence in international league tables of University student numbers. Man in modern society, Fascist, Communist or Capitalist is trapped by educational institutions. These, instead of liberating, now strangle.

This view, which will be developed, belongs squarely in the radical tradition because it criticises education as a tool for creation and maintenance of the undesirable in society. But it goes further. Drawing upon organisational theory, especially in respect of the growth of large institutions, it gives a modern, rather more sophisticated dimension to the traditional debate. And, most important, it does not advance a packaged political solution.

Illich's views on education are not only radical, but complex, and it is not possible, or appropriate, to discuss them in detail. This constant theme is that 'school', by which he means the entire educational apparatus, far from contributing to social happiness, conduces to misery, and, far from making a more just society, exacerbates injustice. It is wasteful of money, and, hardest criticism of all, it fails even to achieve the reprehensive goals it sets itself.

Education, traditionally, has been regarded as an ally in the fight against poverty. Illich contends that, in fact, educational institutions create new categories of poor. The logic of this view is based on the fact that, as educational ladders go higher, there are more opportunities to fail and to fall off. The retort may be made that the reality of life in society is that some must fail so that others will distinguish themselves. Excellence is a relative term, and is part of a process of demarcation. Illich's complaint is that it is a fallacy to suppose that educative procedures produce such accurate categorisation. On the contrary:

> 'In schools, including Universities, most resources are spent to purchase the time and motivation of a limited number of people to take up predetermined problems in a ritually defined setting.'[15]

Those who are not so selected:

> 'are robbed of their self-respect by subscribing to a creed that grants salvation only through the school.'[16]

Schooling, then, is divisive. What happens to the successful? Universities handle these, firstly by co-opting 'the discoverer and the potential dissenter'[17]—incidentally an antique radical source of disgust. Then the institution ensures that 'liberation' is kept at bay. Sometimes, of course, 'reforms' are introduced. But:

> 'most current college-level reform looks like the building of high rise slums.'[18]

The freedom to criticise, which is the University's most vaunted gift is allowed 'only to those who have already been deeply initiated into the consumer society and into the need for some kind of obligatory public schooling'.[19] In other words, the universities encourage their graduates to lead their communities' demands for disproportionate amounts of resources. The graduates, throughout the world, set the standard for others, not in wisdom, or in intellectual excellence, but by the amount they consume.[20] The fewer the graduates, the more 'their demands are taken as models',[21] for example, in Russia, China or Algeria.

The cost of this to the poor is considerable. Because they fail at school, they are disabled. Society, through its educators, does not, however, leave it at that. More money is spent on schools. The curiosity is that the more that is spent on schools, the greater are the failures. It is even more curious that, instead of coming to the rational conclusion that school does not work, the failure phenomenon is presented as a proof that education is 'a very costly, very complex, always arcane and frequently almost impossible task'.[22] Special repair and remedial exercises fail too. The American $3 billion 'Title One' programme failed. There was 'no significant improvement'[23] in the learning of the disadvantaged children at which it was directed. Throughout Illich's critique, there is much which is of considerable interest, not to say relevance, for the adult educator. All that he criticises in 'schooling' is applicable to all adult educational activity. There are, though, several parts of this discussion which merit special mention in this context.

One of these is the implication behind the following remarks about the consequence of a belief that all that is learned, is learned in school, and that extra school learning has no status and is discredited:

> 'children learn most of what teachers pretend to teach them from peer groups, from comics, from chance observations, and above all from mere participation in the ritual of school. Teachers, more often than not, obstruct such learning of subject matters as goes on in school.'[24]

An important tradition in adult education in many countries has always been a concession to the common truth of the point that teachers do not have a monopoly of any category of information (except the narrowly technical). In the best type of English liberal class, on this score, Illich might concede that much more respect is accorded to the complexity of learning situations than he seems to detect in traditional schooling.

A fair question in the light of the considerable criticism Illich makes is why, if schooling, like other modern organisations, fails and does such damage, is this not clear to society? Mainly because teachers have managed to create a mystique. The heart of this mystique is the faith that the reason why they fail is because of the enormous complexity of the task. Further:

> 'the man who questions the need for school is immediately attacked as either heartless or imperialist.'[25]

He might have added another cry, 'academic', which is raised as a response to any proposal for change, even if modest, and seems to be of singular English stock.

Illich's solutions to the problems he discovers are open to such a charge. Schools must be abolished. There should be a:

> 'law forbidding discrimination in hiring, voting or admission to centres of learning based on previous attendance at some curriculum.'[26]

There would be:

> 'an end to the present discrimination against infants, adults and the old in favour of children throughout their adolescence and youth. The social decision to allocate educational resources preferably to those citizens who have outgrown the extraordinary learning capacity of their first four years and have not arrived at the height of their self motivated learning will, in retrospect, probably appear as bizarre.'[27]

He goes on to distinguish one kind of learning situation from another. One of the examples he gives concerns the need to teach Spanish to large numbers of priests in New York. This was done, effectively, by mobilising poor, native Puerto Ricans as teachers, as an alternative to the traditional, institutionalised approach.[28] This initiative should be of interest to adult education agencies, and has considerable implications in all kinds of areas—adult literacy programmes, for example.

Then Illich proposes a complex application of modern technological resources to enable learners to contact each other. There is little point in merely repeating his plan, which is detailed, and may be easily read.[29]

Illich's assessment of the rôle of schooling in society, and the defects of that rôle, is not only of interest to adult educators, but is as important as it should be for the schoolteacher. Freire's discussion is rather more immediately recognisable as relevant to adult educators, partly because he is more concerned with man in society, partly because he wishes adults to be taken seriously, which is a constant theme in adult education, partly because of the method he advances, centring around 'dialogue', and finally because he recalls the radical tradition which pleads for education to be used to expose what is wrong in society. Like Illich, his views are complex, and in this brief account there is only room to recount those which are central to the discussion.

Paulo Freire's main thesis is that man has undergone a process of dehumanization which is:

> 'the result of an unjust order that engenders violence in the oppressors, which
> in turn dehumanizes the oppressed.'[30]

So far such an analysis fits comfortably into the classic radical, political assessment of modern societies. Where Freire departs from the conventional radicals is in his solution. The arresting of this state of affairs does not mean a struggle for power which would transfer the privileges and the means of oppression to the group which was previously oppressed. This, the usual result of a social upheaval, merely replaces one set of oppressions with another. What is proposed is that the oppressed should restore the humanity of both oppressed *and* oppressors. Only:

> 'the power that springs from the weakness of the oppressed will be sufficiently
> strong to free both.'[31]

This process will take place through a 'pedagogy.' It is in his discussion of the nature of this pedagogy that Freire touches on, and develops, so many matters of concern to adult educators.

Freire discussed the inadequacy and unsuitability of traditional education in achieving this aim. The work of the reformer, which will be discussed in the next section, is ineffective because:

> 'No pedagogy which is truly liberating can remain distant from the oppressed
> by treating them as unfortunate and by presenting for their emulation models
> from among the oppressors'[32]

Why is this so? Because of the basic division of societies into the two groups. There is, for example, the very nature of the oppressor culture—'to be is to have'.[33] The oppressor cannot, consciously or unconsciously, 'give' freedom to the others, because this would mean giving away his world:

> 'It would be a contradiction in terms if the oppressors not only defended but
> actually implemented a liberating tradition.'[34]

The situation is such that the oppressor must prevent real inquiry into life, and this prevention is tantamount to violence.[35]

> 'As the oppressor consciousness, in order to dominate, tries to thwart the
> seeking restless impulse, and the creative power which characterize life, it kills
> life.'[36]

A familiar hope is that those who were once oppressed, and have now been converted or assimilated to the oppressor class will understand the nature and the truth of oppression and will try to help. Freire expects little from them. They:

> 'talk about the people, but they do not trust them.'[37]

The status quo is preserved too because of the methods used, which are designed to destroy inquiry. He echoes Illich when he claims that at school:

> 'the students soon discover . . . that in order to achieve some satisfaction they
> must adapt to the precepts which have been set from above. One of these
> precepts is not to think.'[38]

This rôle of the student as 'a non-thinker' is touched upon again when he considers the attitude of professionals. They are the people with a 'world view':

> 'They regard as equally absurd the affirmation that one must necessarily

consult the people when organising the programme content of educational action.'[39]
The education which is purveyed suffers from 'narration sickness',[40] which is founded upon 'a banking concept' when 'knowledge is dished out from deposits'.[41] Those (converts perhaps?) who:
> 'espouse the cause of liberation are themselves surrounded and influenced by the climate which generates the banking concept.'[42]

All of this seems bleak. Freire does, however, propose a scheme for radical change. The key lies in the method—dialogue.[43] This dialogue is dependent for its success on love, humility, faith and hope which collectively form an antithesis to the characteristics of oppression— hate, arrogance, cynicism, nothing.[44] He develops a theory of anti-dialogical action whose ingredients are conquest, divide and rule, manipulation and cultural invasion, and sets against this a theory of dialogical action which relies on co-operation, unity, organisation and cultural synthesis.

As the dialogue develops: 'The oppressed unveil the world of oppression and commit themselves to its transformation . . . when reality of oppression is transformed pedagogy becomes a pedagogy of all men in the process of permanent liberation.'[45] Words will then not be valued for their 'sonority', but for their 'transforming power'.[46] Words will be true, and so the world will be changed.[47] The same point is made by C. Wright Mills when he writes:
> 'In a world of widely communicated nonsense, any statement of fact is of political and moral significance. All social scientists, by the fact of their existence, are involved in the struggle between enlightenment and obscurantism. In such a world as ours, to practise social science is, first of all, to practise the politics of truth.'[48]

It is commonly claimed amongst liberal adult educators that an essential characteristic of their teaching situation is the 'primus inter pares' behaviour and attitude of the teacher. Freire sees, in the development of real dialogue, the logical, desirable, ultimate of this belief:
> 'To exchange the rôle of depositor, prescriber, domesticator, for the rôle of student among students would be to undermine the power of oppression and to serve the cause of liberation.'[49]

Freire, like Illich, is in the mainstream of the radical tradition. Like earlier writers they see a relationship between education and the distribution of power and privilege in society, which means that education, is, for the most part, a pernicious force which maintains the undesirable in society. Since it can be such a strong influence, it ought to be used to change society, by exposing injustice to the poor, women, (although Feminists may feel that Freire does not sufficiently take account of women) or other oppressed groups.

The new radicals, of whom Illich and Freire are especially interesting examples, are not without their critics. Like their predecessors they have been attacked for their views on a number of accounts. They have been accused of being unintellectual, dishonest, unrealistic, and trite. Freire in particular is criticised for ascribing novelty to his methods when, it is claimed, these have been in common usage in adult education for a long time.

Barrow is a representative critic of the radical tradition, especially in respect of modern education. Barrow, *inter alia* claims of radicals that:
> 'To a greater or lesser extent, they are all romantics in the sense of idealistic and sentimental . . . towns and industrialization they hate. They are suspicious of book learning . . . Without exception they overstate, generalize and personalize. They substitute metaphor for argument; they commit elementary logical errors such as interpreting an event as the cause of another simply because it precedes it in time . . .'[50]

41

Such are the reactions of those critical of modern radicals. But the hostility to educational radicalism has many facets. Some of these are debates conducted at an intellectual level, whilst others are more active. I will now set out some of the ways in which the theory and practice of radical adult education are dealt with.

REFERENCES

1. F. F. Korolev, 'Lenin and Public Education', *Prospects in Education*, Vol. 1, No. 2, 1970, p. 48.

2. Extract from the Republic of Cuba, *Report to the XXXI International Conference on Public Instruction* convoked by the OIE and the UNESCO, Geneva, 1968. Published Havana, Republic of Cuba, Ministry of Education, Book Institute, 1968, p. 9.

3. Ibid., p. 9.

4. Ibid., p. 12.

5. Korolev, op. cit., p. 46.

6. Ibid., p. 45.

7. G. Csoma, J. Fekete and K. Hercegi, *Adult Education in Hungary*, Leiden, 1967, p. 56.

8. E. J. Jones, *Some Aspects of Adult Education in Italy*, London, World Association for Adult Education, 1934, p. 29.

9. Ibid., p. 20.

10. *The Guardian*, September 17, 1974, p. 4.

11. Korolev, op. cit., p. 49.

12. *Danish Journal* (Copenhagen, Ministry of Foreign Affairs), 74, 1972, p. 16.

13. P. Manniche (and an international group of writers), *Denmark: a Social Laboratory*, Pergamon, 1969, p. 122.

14. *Danish Journal*, op. cit., p. 18.

15. I. Illich, *Deschooling Society*, Calder and Boyars, 1971, p. 26.

16. Ibid., p. 36.

17. Ibid., p. 40.

18. Ibid., p. 44.

19. Ibid., p. 43.

20. Ibid., p. 40.

21. Ibid., p. 41.

22. Ibid., p. 15.

23. Ibid., p. 12.

24. Ibid., p. 36.

25. Ibid., p. 64.

26. Ibid., p. 18.

27. Ibid., p. 35.

28. Ibid., p. 22.

29. Ibid., pp. 79 ff.

30. P. Freire, *Pedagogy of the Oppressed*, Penguin, 1972, p. 21.

31. Ibid.

32. Ibid., p. 30.

33. Ibid., p. 35.

34. Ibid., p. 30.

35. Ibid., p. 58.

36. Ibid., p. 36.

37. Ibid., p. 36.

38.   Ibid., p. 124.
39.   Ibid., p. 124.
40.   Ibid., p. 45.
41.   Ibid., p. 46.
42.   Ibid., p. 52.
43.   Ibid., p. 42.
44.   Ibid., pp. 62-64
45.   Ibid., p. 31.
46.   Ibid., p. 45.
47.   Ibid., p. 60.
48.   C. Wright Mills, *The Sociological Imagination*, O.U.P., 1959, p. 178.
49.   Freire, op. cit., p. 49.
50.   R. Barrow, *Radical Education*, Martin Robertson, 1978, p. 106.

Chapter 5
Dealing with the Radicals

It is obvious from the discussion so far, that radicalism is not likely to be tolerated by those who hold power. This is as true of education as of any other aspect of social organization. Indeed, a working definition of what is meant by radical could be: 'that which educational authorities are not prepared to allow'.

But the methods used to combat threats to power are by no means homogeneous. Techniques vary from time to time, and from place to place, depending, naturally enough, upon the political traditions and maturity of any particular society. Sometimes the curbing of radicalism is done crudely, and is highly visible; some examples will be discussed later. But sometimes the matter is handled much more deviously. In fact the pattern of resistance to radicalism ranges along a continuum, at one end of which is naked force or violence, actual or incipient. Then there is the allegation that a particular activity is not 'appropriate', or is of a low educational level. This is present in the classical advocacy of liberal education which demands high standards, and rejects social purpose and 'utility' as educational goals. This has often been extremely effective, perhaps because the allegation is not without foundation. In its crudest form this opposition scoffs or sneers at the efforts of those who try to engage in educational activities with groups who, from the traditional point of view, have never been involved in education. But this form of opposition is often, apparently, intellectual and rational, as we will go on to see.

Then there is a very odd, and now rather passé, psychological attack. This questions the *motive* of the radicals, occasionally, in the classic Freudian manner, even challenging the sanity of the participants. But the most subtle pressure, which can only be deduced, and is impossible to validate and difficult to exemplify, arises from the simple fact that people make decisions. It is in the process behind those decisions that the damage to radical innovation can be done. It is always relatively easy to examine decisions which are made. What is more problematic is examining any alternatives, actual or potential, which have been rejected during the decision making process. The business of this chapter is to exemplify some of these means of frustrating what appear to authorities to be educational ideas and practices which threaten the existing social order. A study of these reactions will, in addition, go some way to refining the concept of radical adult education.

At the extreme of crudity, an activity may simply be stopped, usually after an allegation that adult education is subversive. This is a charge which is familiar to adult educators in all countries, but the reaction to the charge by the authorities is a measure of the firmness of democratic traditions. The usual claim is that adult education is being used for the propagation of Marxist ideology. This may sometimes be true, but there are few convincing examples that opposition to Marxist dogma is at the heart of distaste for a policy, since the closure of an adult educational activity is not usually preceded by a rational account of why it is being done. The 'Marxist' label is applied, often unjustly, to activities which, by most accounts, try to examine every aspect of a question. This examination may well criticise existing beliefs, and the allegation of left wing bias is a common reaction.

Such a situation arose in Uganda in 1966, when adult students at a weekend course on national development challenged one of the speakers, who was the Leader of the Parliamentary Opposition:

> 'he raised the issue in Parliament, suggesting that the extra-mural department of the university, which received its money from the Ministry of Education, was encouraging Communism.'[1]

44

There followed a commission of enquiry and the department was directed to concentrate more on 'vocational needs'.[2]

A similar and very far-reaching case occurred in Queensland, Australia in 1939. The W.E.A. was accused of left wing bias, and all financial assistance was withdrawn, both from that organization and from the University department. In spite of much adverse criticism and a plea from Mansbridge himself, the grants were never restored.[3] The consequence was that the provision of adult education in Queensland became one of the slightest in Australia.

Two more detailed cases will illustrate extreme reaction to adult education which displeases. It is not necessary to describe the sequence of events in great detail, since this has been done in the works to which reference is made. What I will do is to discuss these cases in the context of my discussion of the relationship between education and society. One case study is taken from the Sudan, and the other from America.

At the time of the establishment of a W.E.A. in the Sudan in the 1950s, the experience of adult education was, broadly, typical of that of many Third World countries. Resources were scarce, there was concern about illiteracy, the Gezira Board, which was a government agency concerned mainly with cotton, employed full time education staff, and various workers' organisations were in varying degree sympathetic to adult education. There were the beginnings, too, of a library service.

Initial discussions with government, trade unions, and university staff were promising. There was an awareness, stressed by the Minister of Education:
'that the education of the working population was the best guarantee of a
better social, political and economic life,'[4]
This process, it was hoped, would not only result in raising the intellectual level of peasants and workers, but would also be directed at women, whose depressed status can be imagined. Women attended the early conferences, spoke, and expressed the hope that involvement in the proposed movement would be accompanied by moves towards great freedom for them. Had the W.E.A. survived, this task might have led to major shifts in Sudanese society. Women were included in the 'Aim' of the Association which was:
'to develop democratic adult education, particularly for workers, peasants,
women . . .'[5]

The next step was to begin work. To the outside consultant this seemed a model of careful and cautious planning. A firm, if modest, base was established, and was organised by a man with wide experience, including that of trade unionism. The classes which were set up were liberal, lasted a total of 48 hours in all, and were in subjects with a Sudanese bias. They were held in a variety of places, notably in Workers' Clubs, and this connection with workers' organizations was of great value to the infant organization. 'The position of the W.E.A.', its British consultant stated, 'seemed full of promise'.[6]

In November 1958, the Army seized power. Democratic institutions were closed, and workers' clubs outlawed. The W.E.A. soon followed, a process which in some ways was inevitable because of its association with the workers' organizations. The projected first study camp for forty students was 'postponed'. After further interference, without warning, in 1959 the W.E.A. was closed down, and its property was taken over by the Ministry of Education. The International Federation of W.E.A.s protested, but their protest was rejected.

These events not only lost an opportunity for experimentation in the Sudan which might have made it a model for other countries, but it is an incontrovertible demonstration of the fact that totalitarian governments realise that education, especially adult education which seeks to generalize about people's experiences and fit them into an intellectual framework, cannot be tolerated. The prospect of an educated urban and rural workforce,

45

the possible involvement of women, half a population, in the events of a society, can only lead to a questioning of the basis on which the authority of the powerful rests. It is a questioning which may lead to a redistribution of that authority.

The example of the Sudan is not unique, nor are such events confined to countries coping with the problems of post colonial upheaval. An equally interesting case occurred in America. The social setting was different, and the controversy was debated rather more openly, but the result was the same: an educational activity was forbidden.

An area of intellectual thought, in this case Marxism, was under attack. This opposition manifested all the essential objections of the radical to the idea that education is impartial. It demonstrated intolerance, and a lack of trust in the ability of adults to reject what is unintelligible and senseless.

This issue was the nature of the education provided by the Workers Educational Service of Michigan University. In 1948, an economist from the General Motors Corporation alleged that a part time lecturer for the Workers Educational Service (W.E.S.) was teaching 'the Marxist idea of class economics'. The proceedings, from this point, were tinged with rather more sophistication than in the Sudan. The University, for example, felt able to say that allegation was untrue and, more generally, that 'everything that someone doesn't like seems to be construed as Marxism'.[7] The press, however, detected, and condemned, propagandist activity being paid for at public expense. The defence offered does not debate whether or not the lecturer *was* biased, but only drew attention to the custom of the University of employing experts, from many fields, whose expertise could be, and was, marshalled to give depth to discussion.

After a modicum of debate in June, only a month after the economist's charge, the W.E.S. was suspended. This followed a meeting between officials of the University, and the State Governor. The W.E.S. co-ordinator was dismissed and the director of University extension took over his programme. This action led to protests which culminated in the establishment of a Commission of Inquiry into the W.E.S. by the Michigan Committee on Civil Rights. This Commission condemned the cessation of the original W.E.S. work:

> 'because of the opposition to the programme which had been expressed by certain business and political forces.'

This:

> 'led inevitably to the conclusion that this opposition was responsible for the university's action. Unfortunately the Board of Regents and the President of the University acted so secretly as to support rather than to dispel this idea.'[8]

The Department of Extension mounted courses for workers, without consulting them or their organizations, which, naturally, failed to get support. In 1949 the programme was discontinued.

Americans, in the aftermath, drew several lessons from this episode. Concern was expressed by the Commission about leaving 'any large segment of the population out of its educational plan'. One commentator speculated that management should have no more control over workers' education than workers should have over that of management. Another went further, envisaging a possibility that in some situations labour might attempt to suppress management education. Kerrison, in his study of the case, concludes that:

> 'As long as every group may be heard and every opinion stated, neither higher education nor the nation is in danger.'[9]

The radical and possibly the reformer, contemplating the cases which have been outlined, may feel that, in adult education, this is a privilege which has yet to be won. Such oppression they suggest, illustrates a rôle which adult education should play in society—to resist such oppression.

Not all opposition to innovation in adult education is as crude as in these two cases. Throughout the processes which propel potentially powerful ventures in adult education into less controversial waters, there can often be detected one very strong weapon of the opposition to radicalism. This is the allegation that the form of adult education proposed, or practised, is not of a sufficiently 'high' standard. This will be discussed at some length, and cases analysed where the phenomenon is present. These include early university adult education, the Open University, and community education. This is pre-eminently a method of attack employed by some people in universities, institutions which purport to be the repositories of 'excellence'. The concept of excellence manifestly excludes the pragmatic, activist, approach of, for example, the community developer. The claim of the latter that his work is merely a beginning, and that out of it a high standard of educational provision will emerge, is generally dismissed.

University adult education of the classic liberal kind has always been subjected to such attacks. In most countries such provision is not established, presumably in anticipation of the objections that such is not 'university' work. The intellectual paradox in such objections, which those who hold them fail to scrutinise, is that if a university is so important, and its values so precious, then to deny its facilities to the wider community is an absurdity.

University adult education is most firmly established in countries which have an English connection; for example Australia, New Zealand, and those African countries which have not yet destroyed the remnants of the colonial heritage, including a university tradition. Britain has always been the exemplar in this respect, and its university adult educational tradition is mature and well established. Nevertheless, in the early days of extension work, towards the end of the nineteenth century, despite the power and eminence of those familiar figures, such as Lindsay, in the adult educational hagiography, there was predictable opposition to the extension movement. At its most extreme, this utilised what can only be described as a 'sneer technique'.

Marriott catalogues a very heavy assault on the pioneers.[10] He notes a typical 'sneer' in a Pall Mall Gazette Review which complained that Walter Raleigh, in an extension study manual had:

'deliberately ignored his proper public of ambitious housemaids.'[11]

Marriott, in a wealth of interesting material, quotes a more restrained view, but one equally uninformed and hostile:

'If we look at the kind of work which her extension-lectures are performing, we are not quite sure whether, when she spreads the sails to catch the breeze, she is still retaining her hold of the helm. It is one thing to say "I will educate you and I will prescribe what you shall work at" and quite another to say "please tell me what you would like to be lectured about, and I dare say I shall find something to say".'[12]

But Marriott has drawn together even more bizarre fears:

'Though post hoc is not always propter hoc, there was no Jack the Ripper before there was a Toynbee Hall, before sham learning stalked in Whitechapel.'[13]

Such 'objections' certainly raise doubts as to university claims for especial ability to arrive at reasoned conclusions.

The reality is that in this method of attack the issue of 'standards' is a sharp tool, but it conceals a greater fear. This is that activity of the kind proposed by university extension was likely to unsettle a placid population which had been encouraged to hold universities in awe. Those in universities who objected to such activity (and some still do) are the kinsmen of those, described by Thompson,[14] who opposed political change which would lead to a more even distribution of power.

Not all of the opposition to 'extension' of university excellence, whether or not for the purpose of social change, is as crude, or hilarious, as that described by Marriott. Since Newman's *Idea of a University*, which remains a cornerstone of opposition to pressures upon universities to be 'relevant', there has been a steady flow of argument opposing the concept of 'relevance', or the deployment of education as a tool for social change.

Newman's famous case for liberal education is so well known that it is not necessary to repeat it here in detail. But since his opinions have been such a cornerstone in the ideology of education, it is important to recall what, in essence, they are. They are summed up in these two extracts from *Idea of a University:*

> 'Liberal Education makes not the Christian, not the Catholic, but the gentleman. It is well to be a gentleman, it is well to have a cultivated intellect, a delicate taste, a candid, equitable, dispassionate mind, a noble and courteous bearing in the conduct of life;—these are the connatural qualities of a large knowledge; they are the objects of a University; I am advocating, I shall illustrate and insist upon them;'[15]

> '. . . I have been insisting, in my two preceding Discourses, first, on the cultivation of the intellect, as an end which may reasonably be pursued for its own sake; and next, on the nature of that cultivation, or what the cultivation consists in. Truth of whatever kind is the proper object of the intellect; its cultivation then lies in fitting it to apprehend and contemplate truth.'[16]

Paterson, in a closely argued, though contentious, philosophical theory of adult education, is heir to the Newman tradition. He claims that large areas of what passes as adult education (practical classes for example) are not education at all. For him, and he is by no means alone in this belief, adult education means the creation of an intellectual climate, in which people consciously engage in an informed process of self development. Further, when contemplating the notion of social purpose or action, Paterson offers a succinct summary of what are probably widely held views about university adult education:

> 'For those who passionately believe in the desirability of some given social objective there will no doubt always be the greatest temptation to demand that the resources of adult education be utilised as an instrument or weapon in its service. And no one, I think, would seriously wish to dispute that adult education can in many ways make a notable contribution, perhaps an indispensable contribution, to the remedying of many specific social problems and to the general betterment of our social life—for example, in helping to create better industrial relations, helping to improve the quality of family life, helping to smooth the transition between work and retirement, helping to promote higher standards of health and hygiene, helping to reduce environmental pollution, and in countless other ways helping to make the world an altogether better place to live in. However, it is one thing to acknowledge that adult education can incidentally make a notable contribution to the accomplishment of many worthwhile social purposes. But it is quite another thing to view adult education as essentially or primarily an instrument to be utilised in the service of such purposes. This latter conception of adult education is clearly fraught with danger, not only to the deepest values of adult education, but also to the deepest values of society itself.'[17]

48

G. H. Bantock is another recent writer who restates the classic Newman concept of education. He discusses the case of a Zionist school in Palestine which Mr. Boris Ford had described:

> 'He provides us with a description of the workings of the school as an example of the possibility of purposefulness within a framework of freedom. But not any and every manifestation of purposefulness is equally acceptable. The nature of the purposefulness is a vital consideration. The worth of freedom takes its significance from the quality of the order within which it exists. When Mr. Ford reveals the educational purpose of the school, it appears to be an extremely restricted social one . . . "The main task of these schools . . . is to produce good settlers. This means more than at first appears. It means both developing the qualities that go to make a successful Settler, and also confirming the children in their wish to go back to Settlement life at all . . . What makes a Settler, of course, is his socialist (may one say communist?) idealism reinforced by Zionism." '[18]

Bantock goes on to deplore the 'distressing rigidity' of the educational programme with its aim of producing settlers who are Zionist. What would happen to someone who drew other conclusions about the excellence of Zionism than those which permeated the education is not a question which is likely to arise:

> '. . . as all the themes have a distinctly Zionist flavour about them, no child presumably has ever been introduced to the possibility of such an idea.'[19]

It was such deeply held traditions, exemplified by Newman and these other writers, which helped shape the development of the British Open University. When what came to be called the Open University was being discussed as a possibility, there was an assumption that its activities were to be directed at the educationally disadvantaged. Latterly, this term has become confused, if not meaningless; for example, middle class housewives are sometimes categorised as 'educationally disadvantaged'. But in the early 1960s, when the proposal to establish the Open University was first mooted, such verbal acrobatics were rare. At that time educational disadvantage applied to certain people, mainly in the lower socio-economic groups, who had educational potential, and ability, which the system had failed to develop. This new organization was going to address this problem. What its aims were to be, or how it would achieve them, was never made clear. What was certain was that it was going to be an innovative, if not radical, educational force.

This was implicit, and from time to time explicit, in statements made by the Prime Minister, whose support for the venture was crucial.[20] The assumption that it was to offer some kind of a radical alternative to traditional education was confirmed by the fact that the impetus for its development was coming from the Labour Party, and further that Jennie Lee, one of the great socialists of the period, was to be its principal organizational architect. This discussion disturbed conservative elements in the educational world, which is further evidence of its assumed potential for disturbing the *status quo*. The Times Higher Educational Supplement expressed a common fear when it observed that Wilson's scheme sounded like 'socialist idealism',[21] a term which is vague but meant to be opprobrious.

Despite such apprehension, it very soon became clear that the new institution was going to operate, in respect of education *purpose*, as a conventional university. Brian Jackson, Director of the National Extension College, was one who recognised, and deplored, this shift from the adventurous intent of only a few years earlier, to the traditionalism which so quickly asserted itself:

> 'I fear we are in considerable danger of creating yet another university institution for the middle class, and especially for that middle class housewife seeking a liberal arts course . . . the Open University has many splendid uses

... but if it is centrally to reconnect adult education with a major working class audience . . . then it must go and get them.'[22]

In fact, as soon as the Open University adopted the conventions of other universities, the possibility of attracting a 'major working class audience' rapidly receded. The question which was never really discussed was what kind of educational provision would be appropriate for such an audience, if in fact such an audience exists. A very difficult question indeed, and its complexity was, no doubt, one of the pressures which pushed the new institution into more familiar territory. The other, probably greater, pressure was that of achieving academic respectability in the conventional educational world. Hostility to the new organization was commonly expressed even when it became clear that it was becoming a university in the general mould. The sneer technique became a chief weapon.[23] To achieve respectability, the Open University had to demonstrate that its operation compared favourably with that of any other university. And, in a short time, it evolved structures, and courses, which are recognisable, in all important respects, to university staff generally.

This does not mean that the Open University is devoid of novelty. The 'credit' system, which is so foreign in English university education, has been developed, and the teaching methodology is unique. This combines reading and writing with television and radio broadcasting, all of which is underpinned by a tutorial system. These methods have attracted a good deal of attention throughout the world. Admirable as they may be, and however radical as teaching techniques *per se*, they have nothing to do with the fundamental question of the social and educational purposes of the Open University. In respect of method the Open University is innovative, but far from challenging the traditional assumptions about the relationship of education to society, it has contributed to their consolidation.

In this connection, an unusual source of pressure should be mentioned. This came from the teaching profession, and selectors have had to develop a policy in dealing with the disproportionate number of applications from this group. In 1971, a staggering 37% of all students were from 'Education'.[24] Since the possession of a degree makes a considerable difference to a teacher's career prospects, it is hardly surprising that the National Union of Teachers, early in the development of the Open University, expressed interest on this account.[25] In itself, this is a respectable enough, and totally understandable, function. What is, however, hardly admissible is the claim that since teaching provides a notable opportunity for 'upward mobility', the occupation of teachers' parents should be taken into account in measuring the proportion of Open University students who are working class. Nor is it admissible, as is commonly claimed, that teachers who went to colleges of education did so because they were 'deprived' of a university place.[26] This can only be true of those who were trained some years ago. The reason why substantial numbers of teachers chose to go to colleges of education, is that they were insufficiently qualified to gain a university place.

The drift to conventional provision, with a concomitant implication that it has failed to tackle the complexities of 'educational disadvantage', has left the Open University with something of a sense of guilt. Apologists, especially those working within it, generally make some reference to the 'question' of manual workers. It should be noted, however, that these discussions are not very different from those of Oxford, Cambridge or many other universities. *All* periodically reflect upon the low percentage of working class students, and express, with varying amounts of enthusiasm or conviction, a wish to increase it.

Several defences are offered to implicit, or explicit, criticism of the fulfilment of the essence of the prophecy made by Brian Jackson. The first of these is to point out that, in absolute numbers, many students are manual workers:

'. . . something of the order of 15 per cent of our intake come from among manual workers . . . in absolute figures it means over 5,000 people. Anyone who suddenly set up a university for 5,000 manual workers would be regarded as achieving a minor miracle.'[27]

Another defence is that Open University students, because they are mature, are classified in their own right, and emerge largely as middle class. In fact, if the usual university criterion were used, it would be parental occupation which would be categorised. If this were done:

'Preliminary figures from a comparative study of the 1975 intake of Open University students suggest that . . . 52% have fathers in manual occupations. If we were to take into account that these students left school more recently, when the numbers in manual occupations had fallen even further, then this identical figure may even indicate a relative increase in the proportion of Open University students coming from working class homes.'[28]

In any case, it is further asserted, educational disadvantage is too narrowly defined. The equation of such a state with the 'working class' or 'manual workers' is 'not constructive'.[29]

Perhaps the most interesting defence which is made is that manual workers are in some way responsible for their own failure to take advantage of the Open University. This ignores the fact that the institution has decided on the educational packages, and the choice left to potential students is either to accept, or reject. After rejecting notions that the University was founded 'to mitigate social inequality', one writer explains that:

'no "university" whose courses are based on the need for extreme reading of a highly concentrated kind, intensive effort over a very long period, commanding the facilities for peace and quiet, for receiving BBC 2 and VHF Radio, for continuous paperwork and the considerable organizational ability to cope with more than thirty units of work a year, is in any position to appeal to the exhausted manual labourer with poor reading skills, uncomfortable with pen and paper (never mind a typewriter) and unused to textbooks.'[30]

All of this may well be true, even though the people discussed could perhaps regard it as rather offensive. The point is that, through its policies, the organization has created those very barriers, the failure to overcome which now becomes a criticism of educationally disadvantaged manual workers.

The following extract, by the Dean of Arts at the Open University, also implies criticism, while at the same time indulging in attitudes which are both patronising, and curiously anachronistic:

'. . . we could undoubtedly increase the enrolment from among manual workers if we put more resources into advertisement in that area. But the Information Officer is working with a limited budget, and has to husband his resources jealously, and use them cost-effectively. The educational correspondents of *The Times*, *The Guardian* and *The Daily Telegraph* give excellent coverage to Open University matters; their readers are well aware of the University and its potential for them. An advertisement in them will bring an immediate response. Readers of the *Daily Mail*, the *Daily Mirror* and the *News of the World* have often not heard of the Open University and an advertisement there would pass them by. It is my view that growth in this area will be inescapably slow, and will depend very much on propaganda carried out by those manual workers already in the system. But there may be imaginative and inexpensive approaches which might spark off something—a stall at the Cup Final, a letter to the Old Codgers and the like.'[31]

51

Most remarkable of all is the implication, often present in such writing, that the presence of working class students, far from fulfilling at least a residual part of the original purpose, now becomes something approaching a threat:

'The most striking change in characteristics is one that is likely to affect survival, and may well augur ill for the university and the students. The larger number of applicants from working class occupations inevitably means that more students are entering the university with less in the way of previous education qualifications. Behind this lies another significant difference: the number of new students now entering the university who have previously undertaken some form of part-time education has dropped from 80% in 1971 to just over 60% in 1975. The Open University is now starting to reach a clientele "newer" to education, though similar in many other ways. It may have to give it different support.'[32]

There is little doubt that the Open University is of great benefit to large numbers of people, most of whom have had a good measure of educational experience, but have not been especially successful in the strict academic sense. That it took an opportunity to repair what they construe as a defect is, of course, admirable. But it is also the case that the Open University illustrates some of the processes whereby the expectation of radical educational aims, however ill defined, is deflected, and more conventional goals established.

One area of activity which has developed in recent years throughout the world is what is called, variously, community development or community work. Nothing about it is as contentious as its meaning. It is probably true that it is not, on the whole, radical in theory and practice. It is possible, nevertheless, to encounter people who would claim that it *is* radical, in important respects. It is impossible to give any coherent account of the vast and complex range of provision which is included in the generic term community work. The truth is that in some areas, at some times, it is radical, while in other situations it is reformist.

What may be said with certainty is that it is some distance along the continuum from conservation. To some degree, community work seeks to improve society, and by virtue of that task, associates itself with the movement to use education as an instrument of social change. Not only is this immanent in definitions and statements of intent, but it can be gauged from the reaction of authority towards it. These reactions, naturally, vary according to the degree of radicalism of the community work being done, the maturity of the society, and its interpretation of the intent behind this typical definition:

'Community work is essentially about the inter-relations between people and social change, how to help people, and the providers of service, to bring about a more comfortable "fit" between themselves and others.'[33]

Two examples, one from Canada and one from New Zealand, will illustrate what community development is, and the place of adult education in it. The relative degrees of success of the two illustrates the variety of approach in different social and educational traditions.

A straightforward, though very important, and apparently successful, example of the involvement of university adult educators in community development occurred in Canada in the 1920's. It has been called 'The Antigonish Movement',[34] and began in a place called Canso, in Nova Scotia. This was a depressed fishing area, with all the familiar hallmarks which tempt the community developers' inspection and involvement. Housing was poor, prices and wages were low, and there was the usual apathy and resignation which those concerned about such communities try to modify.

A newly arrived priest, Father Tomkins, in 1923 was impressed, in spite of all the manifest disadvantages, with the quality of the community, and the concern of the people over their predicament. His approach, heralding the admonition of Freire, was to trust the people, and to listen to what they had to say. He appears to have seen his rôle, not so much as a transmitter of information, except incidentally, but as a facilitator and an enabler. One of the essentials of community development, if it is to succeed, is that there must be a realisation that the educator's rôle is substantially that of a co-ordinator. There can be no imposed solutions:

'You must have faith that the people will develop their own leaders. You must have faith enough to trust the average man for the general direction of his own activities—if you will expose him to the ways and means of self-help.'[35]

As limited in value as the handing out of packaged information in community development is the mere giving of 'welfare benefits'. There has been a remarkable tendency in social work practice in recent years to regard practical benefits as not only valueless, but dangerous, since to do so results in the client never facing up to the 'real' problem, whatever that may be. In fact, material help can be both of great assistance, and a real necessity, but the most hopeful way of operating is to allow the community to maintain the initiative, deciding what is to be done, and then, with help, doing it.

Tomkins tried to synthesise the views of the community, and encouraged the people to translate their discussions into positive action. Public meetings were held, and informal groups came together in a variety of places—the pier or in a store, where, it may be noted, people tended to assemble to talk anyway. The talk now moved away from mere gossip, because the priest tried to deepen discussion through the judicious insertion of new knowledge. Wherever possible, he introduced the written word as a stimulus. In addition, he performed the essential rôle of the community developer as a mediator, trying to interest wider society in the affairs of Canso, and reminding the latter that it was, in turn, part of that society.

1927 was the 60th anniversary of Canadian Confederation, which was, naturally, a matter for celebration. The Canso fishermen did not feel that there was much cause to join in and, instead, held a meeting, and sent a series of resolutions to their Federal representative in Canada, demanding action. This is, almost invariably, a feature of community work, and is often disastrous. The authorities tend to deplore the marshalling of such complaints and make familiar observations about danger and subversion. In this case, because of the timing, the fishermen received wide publicity, and a Royal Commission was set up. The eventual outcome was the establishment of co-operatives which marketed fish, and established factories.

Another priest took over, M. M. Coady, from the Department of Extension, St. Francis Xavier University, and developed the work throughout the maritime provinces of Canada. In his account of his activity, he sets out an excellent description of community adult education:

'It would be a great mistake to think that such a programme can be solely academic. Such a procedure would be to ignore completely the nature of man. Common people—in fact all people—must parallel their learning with action.'[36]

The result, in his experience, of this essential fusion of cultural, spiritual and economic development was, amongst other things, the creation of a new spirit amongst farmers and fishermen which made them more receptive to innovation—'they now welcome, instead of resist, the government agricultural services'.[37] This movement, which when Coady wrote, was involving some 60% of the families in the area in some activity or other,[38] was, he reminds us, devoted to reform. Improvements can take place within existing social boundaries, since people, given the right stimulus, can:

'determine to reconstruct their lives without resorting to extreme ideologies or revolutionary tactics. The Antigonish Movement is a challenge to the idea that there must always be a submerged portion of the population, the "have nots", the dispossessed people who can never hope to share the good things of life or rise to a decent standard of living.'[39]

The Antigonish Movement has all the ingredients of a typical and successful experiment in community adult education. There was a preparedness to take the experience, feelings and situation of the people in the community as a starting point. There was a realisation that the outsider has a crucial, but non traditional, rôle in events. There was a measure of good fortune. And the ultimate aim, transformation of the community, was not lost sight of. However, the assumptions, the style of operation, and this overall aim, were alien to the main traditions of the adult educator as they have evolved in the twentieth century.

This Canadian experience seems to have been trouble free. The second case, however, illustrates the form and effect of opposition to community development and, more generally, is another illustration of how authorities deal with adult education, which they believe to be a threat. The New Zealand situation was different. Firstly, there were complications of race. Next, due to British influence, the pattern of adult education was rather more settled, with probably less room to experiment, and less tolerance of experimentation.

The Maori people comprise some 10% of the people of New Zealand. Race relations are remarkable in that whilst, naturally, racial differences are a matter of constant public and private discussion, there is a degree of harmony and mutual respect which is rare, or absent, from many other countries with a plural or multi racial population, especially those which are heirs to an Anglo-Saxon tradition. There are several features of New Zealand inter-racial relationships which are exceptional, and in some respects, singular.

There is, firstly, the absence of a generic term of abuse for Maoris which, usually, is an early addition to the vocabulary of the European invader. There is no equivalent to the South African 'kaffir', the Rhodesian 'munt', the Australian 'boong', or the North American 'buck'. On the contrary, and this is the second of many peculiarities, white New Zealanders not only accept a Maori word to describe the whites, but actually use it themselves—'Pakeha'. A third oddity is that Maoris occupy positions of some eminence. There have been Maori knights, university teachers, international rugby players, and professionals of every kind. Despite the incredulity of race theorists and the modesty of New Zealanders, relationships between the races are better than is usual in parallel situations.

Having said that, it is the case that New Zealand is a plural society, with a consequent degree of culture clash which is to be expected, and which has all the classic ingredients. There is, for example, the movement from the country to the city which compounds the problem, since not only does an adjustment have to be made because of cultural discrepancy, but the change from rural to urban society creates more difficulties, the latter problem being complex even where there are no radical differences. There are many other characteristics which are familiar to the social scientist. When Maoris are in towns, they tend to live in the poorer districts. Maori children are less successful at school, predictably 'dropping out' in considerable numbers,[40] and the New Zealand prison population is disproportionately Maori.

It was against such a background that, in 1939, a Young Maori Leaders Conference was held at the University of Auckland.[41] It is worthy of comment that the arrangement of such a conference at such an early date is a measure of the sophistication of relationships in New Zealand society. It was clear that there were defects in such relationships, which were identified, and were considered susceptible to judicious intervention.

54

One of the key problems discussed by the conference was the need to build links between Maori communities which were isolated from each other, and between Maori and Pakeha. It was to adult education that the interested parties looked, and there was laid the foundation for one of the most successful episodes in community adult education of all time, and, incidentally, one of the least proclaimed and discussed. In a report on the conference it was noted that:

'Adult education, facilities for which were conspicuously lacking, seemed to be necessary to develop understanding and give direction to effort.'[42]

The next task was to interest a providing body in the project, and since the universities were the major providers of liberal adult education, it seemed appropriate that they should be approached. After the War, apparently after a lot of persuasion, the first Maori tutor was appointed in Auckland University. One of the most hopeful features of this beginning was that, like any other adult educational venture which is to succeed, it was realised that it would be necessary to consult the people concerned, the Maoris themselves.

The work began, taking as a starting point the main reference points of Maori social and cultural life. Some of the most significant of these are the traditions of oratory, of music, of art, and the central place occupied by the meeting house and the 'marae', the space in front of the meeting house. Through the agency of the university adult educators, these crucial aspects of Maori community life were fostered and, at times, rejuvenated. 1950 was the year in which the Maoris celebrated the sextenary of the coming of the canoes, that is, the arrival of their ancestors in New Zealand. Dr. Winiata, the Maori tutor, and his class members were heavily involved in these celebrations, and one of his groups carved the trophies for the competition prizes. This is a rather striking parallel with the Canadian case, since in both an important national event focused attention on a community, and the work of adult educators in it. At an especially significant time, therefore, the university became intelligible to a large section of the population who had had little understanding of it. The Maori tutors had developed an extremely interesting rôle in this process. They acted as mediators, explaining Maori life to the universities and, in turn, demonstrated to their own people how the universities could help them, and how the two cultures could co-exist, to their mutual advantage. It would seem that the attempt to introduce another culture into university learning which had failed in England, was succeeding in New Zealand. Maori culture was, perhaps, about to be accorded the same respect as Pakeha culture.

After 1950, once the credibility of the university had been established, Maori adult education continued to gain strength. More Maori tutors were appointed, and more students were involved. In addition, the courses and range of activities took a new turn. Maoris began to take interest in the effect of legislation on Maori land, in modern agriculture, and the possibility of developing co-operatives. The potential existed for the establishment of a model of community development, highlighting the contribution which universities could make to it. Not only were the Maori tutors convinced of this, but substantial numbers of Maoris were also. Then, in the early 1960s, the work was stopped.

Universities, not only in New Zealand, frequently manifest a contemptuous attitude towards the wider society. They are content to deploy resources to the education of a narrow age range of people with more or less continuous experience of an education which is designed to prepare for university. Consequently, they regard the community, and its expressed educational needs, with some indifference. This is why most universities throughout the world have no interest in adult education, and why, in some countries, those who do, feel vulnerable. This rigidity in the university's perception of its rôle is sometimes a matter of pride. But as societies become more sophisticated, more observant, and more cynical, the ability of universities to remain unchallenged is likely to be weakened. There is a further, and rather more serious, danger in their rigidity. They may become, in the eyes of

society, of no importance, or even interest. As one New Zealander wrote, very succinctly:
'. . . any argument which prefixes discussion with the assumption that
university standards and, by implication, university rôles are the only fixed
and immutable factors in an age of fluid institutional change, really
invalidates the university's claim to have a larger role as a formative element in
society.'[43]

In recent years in New Zealand, the refusal of those, who were enthusiastic about the work
in adult education which has been described, to be silenced is apparent from the very
existence of the Report on Maori Adult Education. Throughout it, there is a demand for its
resurrection, and for taking the Maoris seriously.

It was the university tradition, and in addition, the university *adult education* tradition
which brought Maori community education to a halt. This tradition was of the English
tutorial class with its three year pattern, with weekly sessions, the production of written
work, and a liberal discipline. Those who saw university adult education only in such terms
expressed uneasiness at the unconventional method and content of Maori work:
'For the first year of the seven years in which a programme of Maori adult
education was attempted, a strenuous attempt was made to fit this into the
tutorial class pattern. For various reasons this proved impractical and for the
next six years the pattern has been both experimental and dependent upon the
persistent request for teaching in traditional arts and crafts. It is now felt that
the period of experimentation is drawing to a close and plans are being made
to settle upon a recognised syllabus of classes and the class forms in which this
instruction will be given . . . The time has now come for the class of serious
students.'[44]

It is clear from this comment, which was not in any way unique, that those who formulated
adult educational policy were not convinced that community adult education was
consonant with university tradition. This general feeling was given a legitimacy by a
Report,[45] which stressed the need for adult educators in universities to direct their attention
to:
'those aspects of adult education which are intimately related to each
university's professional, scientific, and technological programmes of study.'[46]

This Report, which resulted in several major changes in the organization and work of
the New Zealand departments, is relevant to this discussion because it reinforced the
traditional view of university adult education concerning itself with work which could be
appraised as of a high standard. The strengthening of the insistence on university
'standards', and the historical stranglehold of the English model tutorial class structure was
deadly for Maori adult education, at least in the short term, since the debate is not ended.
Predictably, the formal trappings of educational work—registers, syllabus, written work,
and lecturing—are likely to repel those whose experience of such work has been unhappy,
or short. As in England, lower socio-economic groups are not excited by such a prospect.
Apart from a feeling that their work was being devalued, Maori tutors predicted that the
restoration of a classical pattern would eliminate Maoris from adult education. Precisely
this happened:
'Maori language classes for example over the last two years in Auckland
averaged only a six per cent enrolment of Maoris. No Maoris were enrolled in
the usual formal offerings of the Extension Department such as anthropology
or philosophy.'[47]

The Maori tutors, for their part, were assigned new tasks:
'Although Victoria is still fully committed to Maori adult education, the sole
lecturer was recently seconded to the Anthropology Department in his

university for half his working time to teach Stage I Maori language ... Recent trends suggest a stronger interest in Maori scholarship, including Polynesian anthropology and archaeology, and rather less in the social betterment of the Maori people.'[48]

This pattern of events illustrates how subtle the opposition can be when an adult educational activity runs into disfavour. The cause of such disfavour is deviation from accepted tenets about what education is supposed to be doing. When it has a purpose which is designed to 'change' society in either radical or reformative respects, authority is likely to curb it. The radical thesis is that the more threatening an activity is, the more likely it will be that it will be stopped.

Adult educators who subscribe to a programme which is critical of society are likely to be confronted by another phenomenon, which is frequently present when people disagree with those who defend a *status quo*. This has its roots in Freudian and quasi Freudian theory, one of the principal tenets of which is to allege that aggression is normal in the immature, but abnormal in the mature. This premise is, itself, very dubious, but it is the extension of the meaning of aggression which has been of help to those who wish to give theoretical weight to their objections to change. Aggression means the expression of a strongly held point of view which is different from that held by the person defining aggression at that time. Critics of society are not easily persuaded that their views are wrong. A refusal to concede may be noted as aggressive, agression is a symptom of immaturity and instability, and, therefore, those in adult education who advocate radical or reform programmes are expressing 'personal' problems. This device, which reduces opposition, is widely used by those in authority. This may be seen in the adult educational context from an account written by Elton Mayo.[49]

Mayo proposes that students may be 'brilliantly able but unhappy and ineffective'. These 'unhappy individuals' go for subjects as diverse as philosophy, literature, and sociology. Some are scholars, but:

'the scholars of a university are ill equipped to detect amongst their more enthusiastic students those whose very enthusiasm is a symptom of unbalanced development.'[50]

They are, above all, defective in 'social skills'. Mayo then describes his experience in a W.E.A. class in Australia. The 'more moderate and responsible' members sat at the front. The back was 'the haunt of those who represented the irreconcilable extreme Left'.[51] He claims that he came to know them well, and gives a picture of them.

They had no friends, they were incapable of easy relationship with others, they had no capacity for conversation, they were interested only in revolution, and they regarded the world as hostile. In every case, the personal history was 'of social privation in a childhood devoid of normal and happy association in work and play with other children'. One 'drifted into the hands of a medical colleague'. The latter talked about his client's personal history. The client:

'made a good recovery and discovered, to his astonishment, that his former political views had vanished. He had been a mechanic, unable to keep his job although a good workman. After recovery he took a clerical job and held it; his attitude was no longer revolutionary.'[52]

So may the radical be dealt with. His opposition to the established order is explained away in pseudo psychological terms, and his dislike of that which he finds disgusting is a certain symptom of emotional or mental unbalance. Such theorising is attractive because opposition can be disregarded. This approach is widely used in all situations where 'deviant' views are expressed. Freud himself explained away anti-Semitism, anti-Zionism, dislike of individual Jews and, presumably, today, disapproval of Israeli policies, very simply. He gives an example of the things about Jews which inspire hostility and dread: 'the first is that they are circumcized which reminds others of the dreaded castration idea, and of things in the primeval past they would prefer to forget . . .'[53]

Finally, I will suggest the most subtle way in which radicalism may be dealt with. This is through the exertion of pressures, and the making of decisions, which are not always susceptible to scrutiny. The radical would claim that the political activity is to be discovered, not in the provision itself, but in the process preceding it, in the decision making which has led to the formulation of the programme. The analysis of such processes clearly presents formidable problems, since they are bureaucratised, and contain certain assumptions about priorities.

A providing body may set out a programme of activities which is apparently non political in any intelligible sense, and can claim that the courses offered are politically neutral. This is true at one level, in that classes in golf or dressmaking are devoid of political overtones. But the discussion has to begin at an earlier point. The radical sees the political commitment in the processes which have arranged a set of priorities which results in a programme, the core of which consists of courses, respectable enough in themselves, but which contain no vestige of a threat to established assumptions.

Occasionally, as a consequence of sophisticated research concerned with the question of pressures, it can be seen that influences, which are not proclaimed, can be brought to bear on a pattern of events, or on a policy. Thus curbs can be applied to *potential* radical activity. This is a commonplace in the activities of English local authorities, and the examples which occur daily in the local newspapers provide evidence of this. In a report on the work of Environmental Liaison Officers, Hampton gives examples of the inherent fear of criticism which is endemic in those who hold power. The E.L.O., one councillor said, had he been a council employee, 'would have been out on his ear' because he expressed opinions which were critical of council policy.[54] On another occasion:

'the E.L.O. gave advice to the objectors during the hearing of a Compulsory Purchase Inquiry. The local authority were profoundly disturbed by the E.L.O.'s rôle at this Inquiry which was felt inappropriate for a public funded officer.'[55]

These pressures, as has been pointed out, are very difficult to analyse. But they can sometimes be detected in the history of an organization which has always been a vital part of British adult education—the Workers' Educational Association. There are many and complex reasons why the W.E.A. in this century lost such initial radical purpose as it had, and moved into more stable activity. One of these was the pressure to maintain 'standards', which has been discussed. But the invisible decisions to change direction as a consequence of such pressure can also be deduced from the history of the Association.

In the early years of the twentieth century, the W.E.A. issued a statement of policy which set out, in precise terms, what its aims were. It was to be:

'a working class body in the sense that it is an educational expression of the working class movement, and looks on education not only as a means of developing individual character and capacity, but as an equipment for the exercise of social rights and responsibilities . . . to enable the workers to develop their capacities, and to equip them for their Trade Union, Labour, Co-operative and Club activities generally, in the work of securing social and industrial emancipation.'[56]

The W.E.A., then, wished the adult educator to direct his activities to the abolition of that injustice in society which was productive of social unfreedom, educational inequality, and other malignant phenomena which the formulators of doctrine seem to have supposed afflicted if not the entire working class, at least large sections of it.

The genesis of this redemption lay within the working class itself. The W.E.A. was to be the workshop which would forge the new, vital, education which was to reflect working class life. Tawney was one of many who envisaged:

'an educational movement which is stamped with their own ideals and the expression of their own experience.'[57]

Price repeated and developed this theme when he wrote:

'The second great principle underlying the W.E.A. programme and ideal is that the education supplied shall be of the character desired by working class students . . . all that is insisted upon is the recognition of the fact that the working class educational demand has special features consequent upon its being an expression of the working class movement.'[58]

Such policies for adult education are consonant with those of the more relentless radicals. Especially notable is the faith in the special quality of working class experience, and how this will alter the shape of traditional education. Albert Mansbridge advocated this, and pointed out how, when university extension work was increased, universities would gain popular support, would proliferate, and, most attractive argument of all, would accrue more grant.[59] Such arguments were persuasive, but occasionally rather more abrasive comments were made:

'the highest educational facilities in the land shall be accessible to any person who desires them and has the capacity to profit by them. This claim includes a demand for the breaking down of all barriers other than tests of educational fitness.'[60]

One of the most interesting features of the evolution of English adult education, and that of some other countries, is how radicals failed to achieve their task in quite the form set out in early writing. Instead of the W.E.A. concentrating on the working class, harnessing its energies, and articulating its culture, the movement changed direction. It became a remedial agent. Gradually, there was less discussion about the working 'class', and more about the need to abolish discrimination in gaining access to higher education. This was not a higher education suffused with working class experience, but was the traditional higher education which, where it *had* changed, had been modified, not to take account of any lower class culture which was valuable, but to accommodate developments in science and technology. The main theme of the adult educator who subscribed to reform, in several countries, now became the 'demand', expressed by Price, for access. The themes of 'emancipation', social and industrial, figured less and less in policy statements and reflections on activity. There were, subsequently, two major contributions by the reformers.

First, they opened previously restricted avenues to education. Such avenues were confined, traditionally, to those who by accident of birth were propelled into positions of power and influence. Today there is, obviously, more opportunity for other people to progress along carefully delineated channels to peaks of educational achievement with a consequential rise in wealth, status, and influence. The reformer in adult education has made a major contribution to another important related development in this century—the creation of the second chance. Those who alighted from the educational machine are enabled to mount again, and those who never had a chance are given it. This is still not perfect, although the next few years will improve the position; for example by the establishment of the adult's right to a grant for full time study. The opponents of Jude the Obscure are not quite dead, but the assaults on them are due, substantially, to the reformer. This comprises a substantial part of the adult educational tradition and it is here that institutions such as the Adult Colleges, and the Seafarers' Education Service belong, with their contribution to this remedial task.

The reform movement has also created a tradition of liberal education which in England and some other countries is strong. This is the notion that adults can study a subject, not because they want a qualification, but for no better reason then that they are interested in it. This is the kernel of the 'tutorial class' system. Evidence of its significance in adult education is provided by the considerable amount of literature on the subject. Indeed, it is probably true to say that most of the writing on the subject of adult education has been about this liberal education.

The question which now arises is how the direction of reform organizations, of which the W.E.A. is the best example, came to be changed. From a position which echoed much of what radicals proposed, comprising a commitment to developing working class consciousness and channelling it into the main stream of English society and education, the W.E.A. moved to a remedial, reparative position, a rejection of political ideology, and the development of a liberal education which, in turn, is hardly distinguishable from the conservatism of Newman.

To understand this, it is necessary to reflect, briefly, on why interest came to be generated in the education of working class adults in the first place. Probably the main reason was the growth of working class power and influence linked with the interest in socialism, involvement in Parliamentary politics, and the growth of trade unionism. It is never possible to be sure of a person's motives, indeed it is not certain that he can be sure of them himself. And so it is only possible to speculate about the reaction of the emerging adult educational movement to the reality of that growing power. That the W.E.A. felt some sort of obligation to it, is clear, and is frequently expressed. But what should it do?

The trouble at the beginning of the twentieth century seemed to be that the workers were getting power which they could not handle. Indeed, as we shall see, they were conscious of this. To men like Mansbridge the problem was clear, and the solution inevitable. Workers could not handle their new power because they had not learned the rules. So they had to learn the rules, through the process of education. Mansbridge exemplifies this viewpoint in his discussion of the Taff Vale Case. He quotes, evidently with approval, Mr. Bell who reported that the members of the Union:

'"were not sufficiently careful in their selection of the executive committee"; that the tendency seemed to be to elect the members whom he refers to as "irresponsible" and "not the most thoughtful"; but "who have become popular through the exercise of their oratorical power." Upon such a tendency he lays prime responsibility for the damage to prestige and the lost funds resultant upon the adverse judicial decisions in the case. Evidence such as this, from one of the most capable of trade union leaders, must force the hands of those who would promote education. The time is now at hand.'[61]

Education was the answer. It would remedy:

'that lack of thinking power in the rank and file (which) tends to nullify the good effect of such representation, however capable the representatives themselves.'[62]

The radical would probably regard the behaviour of the workers in situations such as Taff Vale as being far from disastrous. He might well conclude that it is the exercise of power in ways defined by others as 'irresponsible' which is precisely the visible sign of the emergence of a working class identity which, allegedly, everyone, including many reformers, looked for so eagerly.

When the W.E.A. was formulating the most appropriate form of education which could be developed in this fluid situation some, like Tawney, as we have seen, seem to have envisaged something which would be peculiarly working class. Mansbridge, however, looked to more traditional sources, and in his faith that such sources would provide solutions, he is typical of the late Victorian reformer. His attitudes to the people who were the object of his concern, and his formulae for their betterment, are reminiscent of, and sometimes identical with, those of a number of men of the age.

There is little doubt of his affection for the people he wished to help. 'Clever roguery' he writes 'concealed immorality, euphemistic lies . . . are not the monopoly of any one class, and certainly not the characteristic of the working class who, on the whole, and I speak of those engaged in steady work, are generous, loyal, and true.'[63] This is the same regard which was expressed by another great reformer, Sir Alexander Paterson, the Prison Commissioner and reformer, who revolutionised the prison and borstal system:

'Borstal training is based upon the double assumption that there is individual good in each, and among nearly all an innate corporate spirit, which will respond to the appeal made by the British of every sort to play the game, to follow the flag, to stand by the old ship.'[64]

In both expressions of faith, and throughout the writing of both men, are two thinly veiled characteristics which help to account for the direction of their reform. Both patronise, and neither trusts the people. This example from Mansbridge is typical, and there are many parallels in Paterson. In a discussion of what would be 'good' for villagers, Mansbridge notes that:

'musicians like Sir Walford Davies prefer the gramophone records of standard music to the cheap and nasty compositions which so often are the only basis for the development of musical taste. A community controlled and not too accessible gramophone should be possessed by every village.'[65]

Since such reformers brought affection and hope, but little trust, to their analysis of the situation, it is not remarkable that they did not look to the working class for the essence of a new education. Instead, Mansbridge turned to traditional adult education. Paterson, when he was looking for a model for his borstal system, and Mansbridge, when he pondered on the most effective form of education, both arrived at the same conclusion: the English public school:

'It is generally admitted that the great public schools are those which are most characteristic of English boy life at its best. Glorying as they do in a splendid tradition, they have always had in addition the opportunity of adapting themselves to new needs.'[66]

In the same way the new workers' education should look to the universities. There was both a demand for more 'extension' on a liberal basis, and for more access to formal degree courses. Very soon the efforts of the hitherto deprived were being compared favourably with the efforts of the hitherto privileged. The 'standard' of work was, of course, that which traditionally had been esteemed. And it was with glee that it was proved that it was a standard which workers could attain. It was reported, and many times repeated, that A. L. Smith of Balliol College, Oxford, discovered that:

'twenty-five per cent of the essays examined by him after second year's work in two classes, and first year's work in six classes, were equal to the work done by students who gained first classes in the Final Schools of Modern History. He was astonished not so much at the quality as at the quantity of the quality of the work done.'[67]

The determination of key early reformers to look to established, traditional education for a model for workers' education, and a pleasing demonstration of success of the kind reported by Smith, widened the gap between radical and reformer.

Any movement away from early quasi radicalism was encouraged further by attacks on the movement at times when it appeared to be threatening the *status quo*. Such attacks were supported by restatements of the belief in education as an objective search for truth, with a concomitant rejection of the idea that education was bolstering any system, or denying the potential for social change:

> 'we must admit that our critics are right. Our classes do not manufacture revolutionary zeal. I say that as the result of having watched and worked in the Movement for fourteen years. But I want to say this as well. It is not our aim to manufacture revolutionary zeal. We have no aim beyond education—the aim of drawing out of a man all that is best and most useful in him for his fellows.'[68]

It is important to note that critics in society have always been quick to express concern at what they conceived to be excesses on the part of the new workers' education movement.

One such occasion was in 1925, when the W.E.A. issued a manifesto[69] in which there was firm discussion about 'workers' control' and 'the creation of a new and juster social and industrial order'. A rebuke from a leading newspaper with accusations that the W.E.A. was part 'of a vast subsidised machinery for the indoctrination of youth' and 'the equipment of street corner orators with an armoury of phrases, catchwords, maxims, and impressive passages from the works of Karl Marx and other socialist oracles'[70] was enough. This criticism led the Master of Balliol College, A. D. Lindsay, to make 'a carefully worded reply which reaffirmed the traditional W.E.A. standpoint'.[71] The essence of this standpoint was a reversion to, if ever there was a departure from, the remedial reformist position as it has been described.

Finally, this reformist activity developed in the way it did because of an intelligible, visible need. A great deal of intellectual and creative ability was untapped, and this was a waste. The opening of educational opportunity, remedial work, and the creation of the second chance, have made a great deal of difference to our society, and the reformer feels pleased with his contribution to it.

The W.E.A. still continues to proclaim the goal of 'educational and social advance'. This is a constant theme in the discussion of the Association in the Russell Report, and in its periodic statements of policy this is clearly set out; as strongly as anywhere in *Unfinished Business*.[72] This document is a good summary of the reformist position at the present time. There is the now firmly entrenched rejection of 'any specific ideology or creed'.[73] In it too is the familiar observation that although 'society has undergone revolutionary changes since the W.E.A. began', it is not perfect. There is:

> 'poverty in the midst of affluence, delinquency and violence, racial misunderstanding and hatred, apathy and alienation in politics, erosion of traditional values by mass culture, the substitution of instant information for thought.'[74]

The W.E.A. seeks to combat these with 'the processes of reason, discussion and tolerance, which are the essence of a liberal education'.[75] Looking back, it is suggested, not altogether accurately, that the W.E.A. 'came into existence very largely to cater for the requirements of those deprived of educational opportunity by the inadequacies of the schools and further education system as it then was'.[76] Therefore, 'the Association must be seriously concerned with the problem of the *educationally underprivileged*'.[77]

Whether the W.E.A. directs much of its time and energy to this latter group is extremely doubtful. There are several factors which militate against its doing so. The main difficulty arises from the very tradition of associating with established education agencies, such as universities. The object was to emulate the style and standards of the universities, and the last sixty years has been full of discussion about 'standards'. This imitation of universities has led to overlapping and duplication, and, more to the point, must, if traditional standards are to be maintained, preclude work with the educationally underprivileged. It is obvious that if the W.E.A. aims to compare favourably with university extension, then its activities have little meaning for those who have defective educational backgrounds. There are, of course, occasions and places when the W.E.A. does involve itself in, for example, the problems of adult illiteracy, but in general it is not altogether sympathetic to the remedial task at a 'low' level. One of the least palatable of the recommendations of the Russell Report was that which, while it was suggested that the W.E.A. should concern itself with the 'socially and culturally deprived' 'work in an industrial context' and 'political and social education', also recommended that the Association should run 'courses of liberal and academic study below the level of university work'.[78]

Unfinished Business is significant too because it introduces a new concept into the debates about the goals of adult education:

'adult education is an instrument of what, in earlier days was described as social or political emancipation and is nowadays known as social or political responsibility.'[79]

This change is manifestly of the greatest significance. 'Emancipation' means something very different from 'responsibility'. It would appear that there is an assumption that emancipation has been achieved, and that now there is a need to handle that emancipation in a responsible manner. It leads directly back to the early days when it was advocated that the new power of the workers had to be used wisely, and with restraint. One of the criticisms made by radicals against reformers is this insistence that education must implant a wisdom which will express itself in behaviour which, because of its restraint, is not likely to create genuine change.

This goal of inducing 'responsibility' is expressed in a definition of adult education proposed by U.N.E.S.C.O. Adult education is:

'concerned with development of personal abilities and the encouragement of social, moral and intellectual responsibility in relation to local, national and world citizenship.'[80]

The concept of 'responsibility' moves the reformer further along the continuum, since there is implicit in it the functional idea that adult education should serve the needs expressed by a society which itself may be taken to be fixed. There is a need for people to act 'responsibly'; adult education should recognise that need, and help to fulfil it. This is far removed from those threats to established society which the early reformers occasionally expressed.

The responsibility theme is one which, surprisingly perhaps, Trade Union educators adopted early in their discussion about educational needs in their organizations. What the formulators of policy have always stressed is the need for education to make trade unionists more competent as trade unionists. This can lead to a very narrow, functional view of what the content of that education ought to be and has led to arguments between those who envisage a quasi vocational content, and those who look not just for competent trade unionists, but for wiser men, and see the former as a consequence of the development of the latter.

The narrowness of the view of officials in trades unions is summarised in the well-known 1921 Report of the Trade Unions' Education Enquiry Committee:

'Trade union government involves an ever increasing responsibility. The administration of trade union rules and regulations has become more intricate and difficult, and each new amalgamation and federation increases these complexities . . . branch records require to be kept with greater accuracy . . . the success of both trade negotiations and strikes is today a far truer measure of the intelligent loyalty of the members and the tact and trained judgment of branch and district officers than it was three decades ago.'[81]

The development of adult education in the way which has been described has had one result which is a constant cause of self examination in bodies like the W.E.A. This is that liberal adult education has failed to make contact with those very people to whom the original endeavour was directed. Very few manual workers, apart from trade unionists attending courses for trade unionists, attend W.E.A. classes. The reason is that the W.E.A. purveys traditional education in traditional styles. The experience of the bulk of lower socio-economic groups in respect of education is that it is distasteful and largely irrelevant. Not irrelevant in the sense that it does not improve occupational skills, although that complaint is made too, but that it is unintelligible, and is not consonant with their experience. The early hope that this experience would somehow be incorporated into education, and would transform it, was never realised and, consequently, education is often viewed with suspicion or indifference by such groups.

This discussion of the Workers' Educational Association is an appropriate summary, in practice, of the theoretical ideas which have been proposed in this book. Here is a major provider of adult education which had, to a degree which is debatable, a radical intent. The organization has survived, (indeed it is very strong), but, in spite of occasional resurgence of radicalism, it has been steered into less controversial waters. This does not mean it is free from criticism from those who deem almost any adult education to be subversive. Nor does this conclusion imply criticism of what the W.E.A. does. It merely insists that the nature of the relationship between society and educators who threaten its stability can be analysed using the theory set out in this book.

I have argued that, in modern times, a small number of theorists and practitioners have tried to 'radicalise' adult education. What has attracted most attention has been the Marxist emphasis, but other dimensions can be discerned and illustrated. The most notable of these is what collectively may be called the awareness of cultural imperialism, which, as I have tried to show, may draw little from Marxist theory, and indeed may cut across it, because of its emphasis on the universal conflict in all modern societies between those who wield power and those who have none.

Looked at against that framework, the Danish Folk High School becomes explicable, in terms of its origin, and its social task. This framework gives greater dimension and significance to the Schools, which are generally recited as monuments to adult education and its success, without quite explaining how or why. It may help to explain too why the Folk High Schools suffer from a crisis of identity, and of aims. It may be added that the fact that they are conscious of this makes them a good deal more sophisticated than adult education systems in post revolutionary societies, especially those alleging a Marxist regime, which are bereft of any convincing overall purpose in adult education, except that of consolidation. Such denial of the reality of the possibility of major change, translated into educational practice, denies those essential ingredients of which education is composed. Socialist, Fascist, and Democratic regimes are *all* prone to demanding of adult education that it depresses questioning and elevates acceptance.

The orientation of this book, it is hoped, will aid the growing development of a body of theory about comparative adult education. This orientation emphasises the need to try to determine, in any society, what the aims of adult education are, to examine the theoretical and practical expression of those aims, and to explore the dynamic relationship between that society and its adult education system.

REFERENCES

1. W. T. Williams, 'Liberal Education in a Developing Country', *Adult Education*, Vol. 42, No. 5, January 1970, p. 311.

2. Ibid.

3. *The Highway*, January 1943, p. 58. *See also* D. Whitelock, *The Great Tradition: a History of Adult Education in Australia*, Queensland University Press, 1974, p. 201.

4. W. E. Styler, *Workers' Education*, Sudan International Federation of W.E.As, 1962, p. 22.

5. Ibid., p. 24.

6. Ibid., p. 35.

7. I. C. H. Kerrison, *Workers' Education at University Level*, Rutgers University Press, 1951, p. 30 (quoting President Alexander G. Ruthven).

8. Ibid., p. 33 (quoting Commission of Inquiry on the Workers Educational Service of the University of Michigan, *Report and Recommendations*, Detroit, Michigan Committee on Civil Rights, 1949, p.5).

9. Ibid., p. 10.

10. Stuart Marriott, 'Extensionalia: the Fugitive Literature of Early University Adult Education', *Studies in Adult Education*, Vol. 10, No. 1, April 1978.

11. Ibid., p. 60 (quoting *Pall Mall Gazette*, 17th October 1894).

12. Ibid., p. 57 (quoting *Macmillan's Magazine*, 61, 1890, p. 283).

13. Ibid., p. 58 (quoting *National Observer*, 11th November 1893).

14. E. P. Thompson, *The Making of the English Working Class*, passim, Penguin, 1970.

15. J. H. Newman, *Idea of a University*, Longmans Green and Co., 1891, p. 120.

16. Ibid., p. 151.

17. R. W. K. Paterson, *Education and the Adult*, Routledge and Kegan Paul, 1979, p. 255.

18. G. H. Bantock, *Freedom and Authority in Education*, Faber and Faber, 1952, pp. 48 and 49.

19. Ibid.

20. Phoebe Hall, 'Creating the Open University', in P. Hall, H. Land, R. Parker and A. Webb, *Change, Choice and Conflict in Social Policy*, Heinemann, 1975, p. 249. This is one of the most objective and scholarly accounts of the development of the Open University.

21. Ibid., p. 251 (quoting *Times Higher Educational Supplement*, 13th September, 1963).

22. Ibid., p. 272 (quoting *The Times*, 25th November, 1969).

23. *See* Pollard's remarks (Chapter 2, note 40).

24. N. E. McIntosh (with J. A. Calder and B. Swift), *A Degree of Difference*, Society for Research into Higher Education, 1976, p. 90 (Source: *University Statistics*).

25. Hall, op. cit., p. 272.

26. J. Ferguson, *The Open University from Within*, University of London Press, 1975, p. 106.

27. Ibid., p. 105.

28. McIntosh, op. cit., p. VIII. *See also* W. Perry, *Open University*, O.U. Press, 1976, p. 140, where the same issue is raised.

29. Ibid., p. 6.

30. W. Van der Eyken, 'The Seeds of Radical Change', in J. Tunstall (ed), *The Open University Opens*, Routledge and Kegan Paul, 1974, p. 29.

31. Ferguson, op. cit., p. 106.

32. McIntosh, op. cit., p. VIII.

33. K. Jackson, 'Adult Education and Community Development', *Studies in Adult Education*, October 1970, p. 90 (quoting *Community Work and Social Change*. Report of a study group on training set up by the Calouste Gulbenkian Foundation, Longmans, 1969, p. 29). Jackson offers a very comprehensive account of the evolution of community development.

34. A full discussion of the programme is in 'Canadian Association for Adult Education', *Adult Education in Canada*, Toronto, Canadian Association for Adult Education, 1950.

35. Ibid., p. 196.

36. Ibid., p. 199 (B. Y. Landis and M. M. Coady, 'The Antigonish Movement').

37. Ibid., p. 201.

38. Ibid., p. 200.

39. Ibid., p. 203.

40. Four-fifths leave school without any qualifications. National Council for Adult Education, *Maori Adult Education—Report of a Working Party*, Wellington, New Zealand, 1972, p. 13.

41. A complete account of these events is in *Maori Adult Education*, ibid., see also Walker R. J., 'Adult Education and Community Development Among the Maori People' in R. Boshier (ed), *Towards a Learning Society*, Learning Press Ltd., Vancouver 1980.

42. *Report of the Young Maori Leadership Conference 22nd-23rd May, 1939*, p. 1 (unpublished), quoted Walker, ibid.

43. A. Williams, 'Continuing Education', in Richard Bates (ed.), *Prospects in New Zealand Education*, New Zealand, 1970, p. 173.

44. National Council for Adult Education, op. cit., pp. 9-10, (quoting *Report of the Auckland University District for Adult Education 1956*).

45. Parry D. H. Hughes, *Report of the Committee on New Zealand Universities*, Wellington, Government Printer, 1959.

46. Ibid., p. 105.

47. National Council for Adult Education, op. cit., p. 15.

48. D. O. W. Hall, *New Zealand Adult Education*, Michael Joseph, 1970, p. 152.

49. E. Mayo, *The Social Problems of an Industrial Civilization*, Routledge and Kegan Paul, 1949, pp. 21-25.

50. Ibid.

51. Ibid.

52. Ibid.

53. D. Stafford-Clark, *What Freud Really Said*, Pelican, 1967, p. 190.

54. W. Hampton, *Providing the Posh Words . . . Two Experiments in Community Participation*, Department of the Environment, 1978, para. 5.7.

55. Ibid., para. 4.16.

56. Quoted by S. G. Raybould, *The English Universities and Adult Education*, W.E.A., 1951, p. 1.

57. T. W. Price, *The Story of the Workers' Educational Association 1903-1924*, Labour Publishing Co. Ltd., 1924, p. 8.

58. Ibid., pp. 80-81.

59. A. Mansbridge, *University Tutorial Classes*, Longmans, 1913, p. 51.

60. Price, op. cit., p. 80.

61. Mansbridge, op. cit., pp. 3-4.

62. Ibid., p. 2.

63. Ibid., p. 61.

64. A. Paterson, *The Principles of the Borstal System*, printed privately circa 1932, p. 4.

65. Mansbridge, op. cit., p. 71.

66. Ibid., p. 50.

67. Mansbridge, op. cit., p. 178.

68. G. V. Portus, 'The W.E.A. and the University', *Australian Highway*, 10th August, 1928, pp. 207 ff.; reprinted in A. Wesson (ed.), *Basic Readings in Australian Adult Education*, Melbourne, Council of Adult Education, 1971, pp. 14-15.

69. This is discussed in A. J. Corfield, *Epoch in Workers' Education*, W.E.A., 1969, p. 32 ff. At Appendix 4 there is a reprint of the complete document.

70. Ibid., p. 34.

71. Ibid.

72. *Unfinished Business*, W.E.A., 1966.

73. Ibid., p. 3.

74. Ibid., p. 5.

75. Ibid., p. 5.

76. Ibid., p. 7.

77. Ibid., p. 7.

78. *Adult Education: a Plan for Development*, H.M.S.O., 1973, pp. 78-79.

79. Ibid., p. 6.

80. *International Directory of Adult Education*, Paris, U.N.E.S.C.O., 1952, p. 246.

81. Corfield, op. cit., pp. 211-212.

Bibliography

Adult Education: a Plan for Development (Chairman: Sir Lionel Russell), H.M.S.O., 1973.

ALLAWAY, A. J., *Thought and Action in Extra-Mural Work, Leicester 1946-1966*, Leicester University (Vaughan College Paper No. 10), 1967.

AMIS, Kingsley, 'Pernicious Participation', in COX, C. B. and DYSON, A. E. (eds.), *Fight for Education: a Black Paper*, q.v. The Critical Quarterly Society 1969, p. 10.

BANTOCK, G. H., *Freedom and Authority in Education*, Faber and Faber, 1952.

BARROW, R., *Radical Education*, Martin Robertson, 1978.

BATES, Richard, *Prospects in New Zealand Education*, New Zealand, 1970. Hodder and Stoughton, Auckland, in association with University of London Press, 1970.

BEGTRUP, H., LUND, H. and MANNICHE, P., *The Folk High Schools of Denmark and the Development of a Farming Community*, O.U.P., 1929.

BENDIX, Reinhard and LIPSET, Seymour Martin (eds.), *Class Status and Power*, Routledge, 1967.

BRADLEY, Phillips, 'The University's Role in Workers' Education', *Adult Education Journal*, Vol. 8, No. 83, April 1949.

CALVERT, Peter, *Revolution*, Pall Mall, 1970.

CAMPBELL, Flann, 'Latin and the Elite Tradition in Education', *British Journal of Sociology*, Vol. XIX, No. 3, September 1968.

COHEN, Percy, *Modern Social Theory*, Heinemann, 1968.

COMMISSION OF ENQUIRY ON THE WORKERS' EDUCATIONAL SERVICE OF THE UNIVERSITY OF MICHIGAN, *Report and Recommendations*, Detroit, Michigan Committee on Civil Rights, 1949.

CORFIELD, A. J., *Epoch in Workers' Education*, W.E.A., 1969.

COX, C. B. and DYSON, A. E. (eds.), *Fight for Education: a Black Paper*, The Critical Quarterly Society, 1969.

COX, C. B. and DYSON, A. E. (eds.), *Black Paper Two: the Crisis in Education*, n.d. 1970?

CSOMA, G., FEKETE, J. and HERCEGI, K., *Adult Education in Hungary*, Leiden, 1967.

Danish Journal, (Copenhagen, Ministry of Foreign Affairs), 74, 1972.

DAVIS, Keith, *Human Relations at Work: the Dynamics of Organisational Behaviour*, New York, McGraw-Hill, 1967.

DEEM, R., *Women and Schooling*, Routledge and Kegan Paul, 1978.

ELIOT, T. S., *Essays Ancient and Modern*, Faber & Faber, 1949.

EMERSON, Ralph Waldo, *Essays, First and Second Series*, New York, Macmillan, 1885.

FERGUSON, J., *The Open University from Within*, University of London Press, 1975.

FLEMING, H., *Education through Settlements*, Birkenhead, Beechcroft Bulletin No. 2, 1922.

FLETCHER, C. and THOMPSON, N., *Issues in Community Education*, Falmer Press, 1980.

FREIRE, P., *Pedagogy of the Oppressed*, Penguin, 1972.

GAVRON, Hannah, *The Captive Wife*, Routledge and Kegan Paul, 1966.

GROSS, Edward, 'The Definition of Organizational Goals', *British Journal of Sociology*, Vol. XX, No. 3, September 1969.

HALL, D. O. W., *New Zealand Adult Education*, Michael Joseph, 1970.

HALL, P., 'Creating the Open University' *in* HALL, P., LAND, H., PARKER, R. and WEBB, A., *Change, Choice and Conflict in Social Policy*, q.v.

HALL, P., LAND, H., PARKER, R. and WEBB, A., *Change, Choice and Conflict in Social Policy*, Heinemann, 1975.

HAMPTON, W., *Providing the Posh Words . . . Two Experiments in Community Participation*, Department of the Environment, 1978.

Highway, January 1943, Workers' Educational Association.

HIRSCH, Walter, *see* ZOLLSCHAN, G. K.

HOGGART, Richard, *The Uses of Literacy*, Penguin, 1969.

HORRABIN, J. F. and W., *Working Class Education*, Labour Publishing Company, 1924.

HUGHES, Parry D. H., *Report of the Committee on New Zealand Universities*, Wellington, Government Printer, 1959.

ILLICH, I., *Deschooling Society*, Calder and Boyars, 1971.

International Directory of Adult Education, Paris, U.N.E.S.C.O., 1952.

'IVAN THE FOOL', *Fellowship*, Vol. IV, No. 8, March 1918, ed. F. Sinclaire; reprinted in WESSON, A., *Basic Readings in Australian Adult Education*, q.v.

JOHNSON, Chalmers, *Revolution and the Social System*, U.S.A. Hoover Institute Press, 1964.

JOHNSTONE, J. W. C. and RIVERA, R. J., *Volunteers for Learning: a study of the educational pursuits of American adults*, Chicago, National Opinion Research Centre, Monographs in Social Research, Aldine Publishing Company, 1965.

JONES, E. J., *Some Aspects of Adult Education in Italy*, London, World Association for Adult Education, 1934.

KELLY, T., *A History of Adult Education in Great Britain*, Liverpool University Press, 1962, reprinted 1970.

KERRISON, I. C. H., *Workers' Education at the University Level*, Rutgers University Press, 1951.

KOCH, H., *Grundtvig*, Antioch, 1952.

KOROLEV, F. F., 'Lenin and Public Education', *Prospects in Education*, Vol. 1, No. 2, 1970.

LANDIS, B. Y. and COADY, M. M., 'The Antigonish Movement', *in* CANADIAN ASSOCIATION FOR ADULT EDUCATION, *Adult Education in Canada*, q.v. Toronto, 1950.

LENSKI, Gerhard E., *Power and Privilege*, New York, McGraw-Hill, 1966.

LINDHARDT, P. G., *Grundtvig—an Introduction*, S.P.C.K., 1951.

LIVINGSTONE, R. W., 'The Danish People's High Schools: a Reply', *Adult Education*, Vol. XIV, No. 3, March 1942.

LIVINGSTONE, R. W., *Future in Education*, C.U.P., 1941.

LIVINGSTONE, R. W., *Greek Ideals and Modern Life*, Oxford University Press, 1935.

LOCKWOOD, David, 'Social Integration and System Integration', *in* ZOLLSCHANG, K., and HIRSH, Walter (eds.), *Exploration in Social Change*, q.v.

LOVETT, T., *Adult Education, Community Development and the Working Class*, Ward Lock, 1975.

LOWE, John, *Adult Education in England and Wales: a Critical Survey*, Michael Joseph, 1970.

McINTOSH, N. E. (with J. A. CALDER and B. SWIFT), *A Degree of Difference*, Society for Research into Higher Education, 1976.

MANNICHE, P. (and an international group of writers), *Denmark: a Social Laboratory*, Pergamon, 1969.

MANSBRIDGE, A., *The Kingdom of the Mind*, Meridian Press, 1946 (originally published by E. M. Dent, 1944).

MANSBRIDGE, A., *University Tutorial Classes*, Longmans, 1913.

MARRIOTT, Stuart, 'Extensionalia: the Fugitive Literature of Early University Adult Education', *Studies in Adult Education*, Vol. 10, No. 1, April 1978.

MAYO, E., *The Social Problems of an Industrial Civilisation*, Routledge and Kegan Paul, 1949.

MAZZINI, Giuseppi, *The Duties of Man and Other Essays, by Joseph Mazzini*, London, 1912.

MERTON, Robert K., 'Social Structure and Anomie', *American Sociological Review*, Vol. 3, 1938.

MILLAR, J. P. M., *The Trained Mind: Trained for What?*, National Council of Labour Colleges, n.d. circa 1927.

MILLETT, Kate, *Sexual Politics*, Hart Davis, 1971.

MILLS, C. Wright, *The Sociological Imagination*, O.U.P., 1959.

MOORE, Barrington, *Social Origins of Dictatorship and Democracy*, Penguin, 1967.

MORRIS, H., 'The Danish Folk High School Myth', *Adult Education*, Vol. XIV, No. 2, December 1941.

NATIONAL COUNCIL FOR ADULT EDUCATION, *Maori Adult Education—Report of a Working Party*, Wellington, New Zealand, 1972.

NATIONAL INSTITUTE OF ADULT EDUCATION, *Adult Education—Adequacy of Provision*, National Institute of Adult Education, 1970.

NEWMAN, J. H., *Idea of a University*, Longmans, Green and Co., 1891.

NEWSOM, J., *The Education of Girls*, Faber and Faber, 1948.

NOKES, P. L., *The Professional Task in Welfare Practice*, Routledge and Kegan Paul, 1967.

OTTAWAY, A. K. C., *Education and Society*, Routledge, 1953.

PAINE, Thomas, *Rights of Man. Being an Answer to Mr. Burke's Attack on the French Revolution*, London, 1930.

PARSONS, Talcott, 'The Distribution of Power in American Society', *World Politics*, Vol. 10, October 1957.

PASHLEY, B. W., *University Extension Reconsidered*, Leicester University (Vaughan College Paper No. 11), 1968.

PATERSON, R. W. K., *Values, Education and the Adult*, Routledge and Kegan Paul, 1979.

PERRY, W., *Open University*, O.U. Press, 1976.

POLLARD, Arthur, 'O and A Level: Keeping up the Standards', in COX, C. B. and DYSON, A. E. (eds.), *Black Paper Two: the Crisis in Education*, q.v. the Critical Quarterly Society, n.d. 1970?

PORTUS, G. V., 'The W.E.A. and the University', *Australian Highway*, 10th August, 1928; reprinted in WESSON, A. (ed.), *Basic Readings in Australian Adult Education*, q.v.

PRICE, T. W., *The Story of the Workers' Educational Association 1903-1924*, Labour Publishing Co. Ltd., 1924.

RAYBOULD, S. G., *The English Universities and Adult Education*, W.E.A., 1951.

RAYBOULD, S. G., *University Extra-Mural Education in England 1945-62: a Study in Finance and Policy*, Michael Joseph, 1964.

RECONSTRUCTION, MINISTRY OF, *Final Report of the Adult Education Committee*, H.M.S.O., 1919.

REIMER, E., *School is Dead*, Penguin, 1971.

RIESMAN, David, *The Lonely Crowd*, New York, Yale University Press, 1953.

Report of the Young Maori Leadership Conference 22nd-23rd May, 1939 (unpublished).

REPUBLIC OF CUBA, *Report to the XXXI International Conference on Public Instruction*, convoked by the O.I.E. and the U.N.E.S.C.O., Geneva, 1968, Havana, Republic of Cuba, Ministry of Education, Book Institute, 1968.

RIVERA, R. J., *see* JOHNSTONE, J. W. C.

RORDAM, T., *The Danish Folk High Schools*, Det Danske Selskab, 1965; rev. ed. 1980.

ROUSSEAU, J. J., *Emile*; trans. B. Foxley, Dent (Everyman), 1948.

RUSKIN, J., *Sesame & Lilies*, George Allen 1903.

SARUP, M., *Marxism and Education*, Routledge and Kegan Paul, 1978.

SMELSER, Neil J., *Theory of Collective Behaviour*, New York, Routledge, 1962.

SPIVEY, Donald, *Schooling for the New Slavery: Black Industrial Education 1868-1915*, Greenwood Press, 1978.

STAFFORD-CLARK, D., *What Freud Really Said*, Pelican, 1967.

STYLER, W. E., *Workers' Education*, Sudan International Federation of W.E.As, 1962.

SWANSON, Guy E., *Social Change*, Illinois, Glenview, 1971.

TAWNEY, R. H., *The Radical Tradition*, Penguin, 1966.

THOMPSON, E. P., *The Making of the English Working Class*, Penguin, 1970.

TUNSTALL, J. (ed.), *The Open University Opens*, Routledge and Kegan Paul, 1974.

The Tutor's Bulletin (Association of Class Tutors).

Unfinished Business, W.E.A., 1966.

VAN DER EYKEN, W., 'The Seeds of Radical Change', *in* TUNSTALL, J. (ed.), *The Open University Opens*, q.v.

WALKER, R. J., *Adult Education and Community Development among the Maori people*, in Boshier R. (ed), *Towards a Learning Society*, Learning Press Ltd., Vancouver, 1980.

WALLER, R. D. (ed.), *A Design for Democracy*, Parrish, 1956.

WESSON, A. (ed.), *Basic Readings in Australian Adult Education*, Council of Adult Education, Melbourne, 1971.

WHITEHEAD, A. N., *The Aims of Education*, Benn, 1962.

WHITELOCK, D., *The Great Tradition: a History of Adult Education in Australia*, Queensland University Press, 1974.

WILLIAMS, A., 'Continuing Education', *in* BATES, Richard (ed.), *Prospects in New Zealand Education*, q.v.

WILLIAMS, W. T., 'Liberal Education in a Developing Country', *Adult Education*, Vol. 42, No. 5, January, 1970.

WILTSHIRE, H., TAYLOR, J. and JENNINGS, B., *The 1919 Report: the Final and Interim Reports of the Adult Education Committee of the Ministry of Reconstruction 1918-1919*, Department of Adult Education, University of Nottingham, 1980.

WOLLSTONECRAFT, M., *Vindication of the Rights of Women*, 1972.

WOOLF, Virginia, *A Room of One's Own*, Hogarth Press, 1949.

WORKERS' EDUCATIONAL ASSOCIATION, *Unfinished Business*, 1966.

ZOLLSCHANG, G. K. and HIRSCH, Walter (eds.), *Exploration in Social Change*, Routledge and Kegan Paul, 1964.

Index